LESSONS IN
BUOYANCY

LESSONS IN BUOYANCY

LETTING GO *of the* PERFECT PROVERBS 31 WOMAN

KATHY VICK

 Revell
Grand Rapids, Michigan

© 2004 by Kathy Vick

Published by Fleming H. Revell
a division of Baker Book House
P.O. Box 6287, Grand Rapids, MI 49516-6287
www.bakerbooks.com

Printed in the United States of America

Library of Congress Cataloging-in-Publication Data
Vick, Kathy, 1956-
   Lessons in buoyancy : letting go of the perfect Proverbs 31 woman / Kathy Vick.
        p.   cm.
    ISBN 0-8007-5907-9 (pbk.)
       1. Christian women—Religious life. 2. Bible. O.T. Proverbs XXXI—Criticism, interpretation, etc. I. Title.
   BV4527.V53 2004
   248.8'.43—dc22   2004000737

This book is for my parents,
Marjorie and David Boice,
who taught me that
all of life is an adventure

CONTENTS

A wife of noble character who can find?
    She is worth far more than rubies.
Her husband has full confidence in her
    and lacks nothing of value.
She brings him good, not harm,
    all the days of her life.
She selects wool and flax
    and works with eager hands.
She is like the merchant ships,
    bringing her food from afar.
She gets up while it is still dark;
    she provides food for her family
    and portions for her servant girls.
She considers a field and buys it;
    out of her earnings she plants a vineyard.
She sets about her work vigorously;
    her arms are strong for her tasks.
She sees that her trading is profitable,
    and her lamp does not go out at night.
In her hand she holds the distaff
    and grasps the spindle with her fingers.
She opens her arms to the poor
    and extends her hands to the needy.
When it snows, she has no fear for her household;
    for all of them are clothed in scarlet.

continued on next page

She makes coverings for her bed;
  she is clothed in fine linen and purple.
Her husband is respected at the city gate,
    where he takes his seat among the elders of the
      land.
She makes linen garments and sells them,
    and supplies the merchants with sashes.
She is clothed with strength and dignity;
    she can laugh at the days to come.
She speaks with wisdom,
    and faithful instruction is on her tongue.
She watches over the affairs of her household
    and does not eat the bread of idleness.
Her children arise and call her blessed;
    her husband also, and he praises her:
"Many women do noble things,
    but you surpass them all."
Charm is deceptive, and beauty is fleeting;
    but a woman who fears the LORD is to be praised.
Give her the reward she has earned,
    and let her works bring her praise at the city gate.

PROVERBS 31

INTRODUCTION

A Noble Character —
Who Can Find?

ONE AFTERNOON IN June, my friend and I sat in my living room talking about the possibility of writing this book.

"I have nothing to say," I told her. "My kids are not grown . . . I make a lot of mistakes . . . I lose myself in my family sometimes, and I have only been a stepmother for five years . . . I haven't figured it all out—how to be a good wife and better mother . . . I'm just surviving here."

She asked me if I would show her what I had been writing. I read her a single page from my journal about meeting a woman who asked me what I did. When I replied that I was a stay-at-home mom, she pressed, "No, what do you do, *really?*"

In retrospect, what I read was a pretty angry entry. I felt judged for my choice to stay home to tend to the needs of my children and my husband. I felt frowned upon, like I should be more than this center that helps hold my home, our kids, and our family together—like these things couldn't possibly consume me. But they did, and beneath all the anger was my frustration and fear, all my doubts that maybe I really wasn't

11

enough—enough mom, enough wife, enough me, enough of the woman God created to go forth and conquer.

"That's it," my friend said. "That's what I want you to write about."

I want you to know I thought she was crazy. Who's going to read a book about a woman who is surely imperfect and possibly nuts?

When I became a stepmother, I had grandiose ideas about saving my kids. Of course, I don't have that power, but that didn't keep me from trying. I thought love and sheer will could conquer every problem my kids would face. Five years and thousands of dollars in counseling fees later, I know there are things I just cannot do. I know I will never bake enough cookies or listen enough, and I know there is nothing I can do to make my kids' pain evaporate. I know that I can't be enough—on my own—and somewhere in my heart I acknowledge that for all my overachieving, the real gift and lesson is that God uses imperfect, unbalanced women every day to alter hearts and the landscapes of our families.

I know I can't achieve perfect balance. I'm beginning to think none of us is supposed to, and none of us has—not even that spiritual supergirl, the Proverbs 31 woman. In fact, the more I think about her, the more real she becomes to me: She brings. She selects. She provides. She considers and sets about; she sees and opens her arms, makes coverings and linens, is clothed, and speaks. She watches.

Then—get this—I realized what I'd been missing: She *is*.

She is a part of who God wants every woman to be, a woman after his heart—and I'm convinced God has a much larger agenda than we can see at work in our lives. His plan is to give us buoyancy in the midst of motion, calm in a sea of stress and an ocean of disappointment. He wants us to be able to operate as though we have a net to catch us when we fall and a buoying hope and optimism that holds us up regardless of circumstance. This is a far greater goal than just balance. Buoyancy gives us freedom to take the road less traveled and to count on the laws of gravity, which God so graciously provides, to always keep us centered and on course.

I say this admitting that in the stress, I've dog-paddled without grace. I've felt very lonely as a mother and often felt swept into an undertow of fear—afraid most of all to share these admissions, even though my motives were good and perhaps even protective of those I love.

So I wrote this book for me and for all of you like me who need reminding that God has our pictures in his wallet. He loves us. He wants us to love ourselves and each other. He sends us messengers like the Proverbs 31 woman to remind us that we need to tell the truth about mothering and being a good wife, a creative worker, and a dedicated daughter. We need to take care of ourselves and our dreams.

As for the incident that spawned that angry journal entry and this book: I am eternally grateful for the woman who asked me, "No, what do you do, really?"

Without her I may never have reintroduced myself to Proverbs 31, and I might still be sitting at home, thinking I had nothing to say.

1

FLOAT

Lessons in Faith

She can laugh

Float like a butterfly, sting like a bee.

MUHAMMAD ALI

I CRIED THE day I had to jump into the deep end. I stood staring at the bottom, praying for some form of miraculous intervention, as the rest of my class waited, arms folded and shivering. My head itched under the thick, white, rubber bathing cap, and I had a churning feeling in my stomach that made me fear my breakfast was going to reach the bottom of the pool before I could.

My swim instructor called out, "I promise you will float."

Every inch of me in my one-size-too-small swimsuit wanted to believe that was true. Still I doubted.

When I finally left the safety of the edge and plunged down into the aqua depths of the YWCA pool, my heart was pounding like a hammer. I touched the bottom and then, on some instinct I didn't know was in me, pushed off . . . and broke the surface.

I bobbed there a minute, stunned.

Somehow I had floated to the top.

What I learned that day was that my life, like my swimming, counts on certain laws of gravity and flotation.

A lot of us have forgotten this. We work so hard to keep our heads above water that we've neglected these seemingly insignificant forces of grace at work in our lives. We yearn to be extraordinary at the trade of mothering, yet can't stop feeling small in comparison to the woman next to us. We burn the midnight oil to bake three hundred cookies for a child's class and end up burning out when it comes to our own futures. We doubt too often our own value as we fill our time with the everyday activities of being supermom, superwife, superhuman with superstrength.

Five years ago I became a wife and a mother to two teenagers. The difficulty level of my experience to date is equivalent to that of nailing jelly to a tree. My home is filled with my daughter and her hormonal, inane, giggling, fifteen-year-old friends (enough said) and my nineteen-year-old son, who equates coolness to one-syllable answers and a lack of hygiene. Recently I told my mother there are days I just want to get into the car and drive to a motel.

Instead I have read books, listened to tapes, and joined moms online. I've taken magazine self-tests and logged hours of *Oprah* only to discover that the problem is not something I can fix. The dilemma is the whole Mommy System.

The common litany about motherhood is a lot of false advertising at best, and I'm still trying to unravel the truth. The truth is, I don't find joy in clean bathrooms and neatly folded laundry. I don't revel in discovering yet another family-pleasing recipe. The idea that these things define me or my future makes me question my own sanity and feel like I'm secretly applying for sainthood for enduring it all. It brings to mind the image of the robot from the original *Lost in Space,* its arms flying up in the air—"Warning! Danger, Will Robinson! Danger!"

Like balancing a grizzly on a pine cone, becoming a mother at age forty-one has defied gravity, logic, and the idea of comfort or perfection. It has rocked my world and taken me to the edge of myself, throwing around my ego like one of those electric bulls, testing my poise and stamina. It has lacked grace and poise, and maybe that is its gift, for coming to the end of myself has replaced my lesser imagination with a more real truth.

That truth is this: A woman's life, especially in motherhood, is one gigantic act of buoyancy that requires a core of faith. It means believing that the same promise God made to Noah is offered to me: You will float. No matter how high the water or how insurmountable the task, if my security is in God, it's a sure thing.

Buoyancy in every part of my life will depend on this knowledge and the faith at my core, the God at my center. Buoyancy will draw from all the lessons God has taught me: lessons of laughter; lessons of strength and hope along the folds of my history and the fabric of my character. Buoyancy will take time, and it will change me in minute and profound ways—forever.

Of course, first I have to go to the deep end and jump. The miracle of buoyancy, of learning to float, cannot be experienced unless we're in the water up to our necks and wondering where the bottom went.

This was where I started—in over my head, looking for the edge of the pool.

I heard my daughter Andrea relating our family history to a friend: "Most moms wait nine months for a kid," she said. "My mom waited for me in court."

18

She is right. At forty-one, never married before, I fell in love with a man who had two children, and I fell in love with them too. After we married and experienced a series of anxious events, we hoped the children could come to live with us. We dreamed of making their lives beautiful and right, of loving them and them loving us back.

So I waited six months to have my entire life changed forever.

Most moments I'm remarkably grateful. I realize how my children have increased my boundaries, affirmed my life, and put me on a path with other amazing women—moms. I love my kids, and though they often see me waffling, they know they were worth fighting for and that I am willing to wait.

Regardless of how you become a mother, one of the keys is this waiting. You wait to get them. You wait to make some show of yourself. You wait for them to grow, and then at some point (and these are the moments that moms rarely talk about but all experience) you can't wait to see the last box of size 13 Converse and rock band T-shirts move out. All the endless waiting often seems like an unfair trade. In this experience called motherhood, the wind is fierce, the water is treacherous, and there's little room for error. These are the days you make mistakes, lots of them, like yelling instead of listening, freaking out instead of breathing in, and spinning in frustration instead of praying for buoyancy so you can stand in God's grace.

Thank goodness for the knowledge that whatever waiting period I'm in, I'm not on unknown ground. There's a well-known woman who's been here too, a woman who never flinched. She is a wife and mother whose path is ancient and tried. She is referred to by number, which I imagine her saying like James Bond: *Thirty-One.* Proverbs Thirty-One.

P31's example has been thrown in my path a zillion times, like an obstacle, because the traditional view of her, the rumor of the centuries, is that she never faltered. She's veritable perfection, a woman who never sleeps and never slacks and who probably never ate croutons out of the box for lunch.

Let's get real. Recently I watched one of those perfect homemakers on a TV show make padded coat hangers by hand—five of them. I consider this a form of torture. Not only do I not want to make padded coat hangers, I don't know of any mom who does.

If P31 is to be one of my mentors, she must lead me toward a *bona fide* and rich horizon, and I need to believe she's traveled beyond that horizon and knows what's at the finish line. The secrets she reveals must be worth the trip. She needs to leap off the page of my Bible and become real to me. I need to know she felt bruises when she tripped over the Frisbee in the hallway, cried tears when her kids misunderstood her, and clipped coupons for pizza delivery in case the dinner burned.

In their book *The Sacred Romance*, authors John Eldredge and Brent Curtis tell us that we have an internal story being written in our hearts. This story has a beginning and an end, and God is the author. He is crafting a flesh-and-blood redemptive drama in us, and the plot has a sole objective: To bring us home to him, to ourselves, and to the purpose he's designed us for.

My story did not begin five years ago when I became a wife and a mom. It began forty-seven years ago when God knit me together; it continued when my mother named me Kathleen after her favorite Sunday school teacher and later when, at seven years old, after a particularly moving sermon, I decided to baptize the farm cats in the basement of my grandparents' house. It began and continues as it will end, with lessons from God and those he places in my path. Every day he writes a little more, and every day I am more certain the ending will be a good one.

I am certain because I can look at the story today and see he's a master of plot and pacing. I am witness to all the twists and turns my life has taken to create drama and intrigue, levity and lessons. One such lesson began when I was eleven and my parents decided we should learn to sail. We bought a seventeen-foot wooden boat with a centerboard that pulled up to sail the shallow channels of the Chesapeake Bay. We spent many afternoons sailing from one shore to the next, eating hand-packed lunches, and searching the beaches for rocks and shells. Before you think this sounds too idyllic, there was one downside to these trips: a complete lack of bathroom facilities.

My father was either very brave or a masochist to have brought three women on a boat with no bathroom (head), and we had to quickly learn to be resourceful. Still, there was mutiny among us for a bathroom, and so my parents bought a new vessel, one with a head, a cabin, and a keel.

The keel was new to us. Our father showed it to us and explained how this long, heavy, fin-shaped protrusion on the bottom of the boat keeps it afloat and in line, just as the wings do for an airplane. Then he gave us the experience of an example. He brought the boat to a heel, which angled the boat to a good fifteen degrees in the water. My sister and I scrambled to the high side and screamed our heads off with terror. Although my father, who was from a family of men, often underestimated how we would react to danger, he had become adept at lengthy explanations to reassure his daughters. Calmly he told us, "The keel is weighted to give the boat perfect balance, and it keeps us headed in the right direction."

My sister and I took this in; the next time we were heeled over, we clung with our toes over the opposite side of the cockpit and pressed our backs against the rail, squealing in delight. We had forgotten our fear, knowing we had the keel under us. From then on, even when the wind pressed us to the waves and the sails strained above our heads, we never doubted our father's words.

Those words echo in my head as I traverse the deep waters of motherhood. I've decided I need to be sure of the weight of my keel. I need to listen to my heavenly Father's words of assurance as I lean against the rail, toes tucked in. What is at my center will still determine my ability to keep on sailing.

I believe my heavenly Father, and I want to be fearless. I believe that he has my back. Still, I am often the girl by the pool waiting to dive into the deep end, stomach churning, shivering in the suit that doesn't quite cover my backside. I am both brave and cowardly, solid and fluid; I am heeled over, straining against the wind, my ribs creaking, the shrouds singing shrill and loud.

It's this quirky sense of balance that leads me to consider that God intends us to float. He wants us to know that life's pressures can be displaced by the weight of who we are and what he has put at our core. He wants us to finally give up on the idea of perfect balance and embrace the gift of buoyancy and faith in our keel. There is freedom in this realization, like having God walk into your kitchen and tell you that regardless of what happens next you won't be overwhelmed, assuring you that he made you for a much larger purpose than you will ever be able to comprehend.

I believe this is the definition of the buoyancy that God call us to. It is edgy, imperfect buoyancy that requires both faith in the unseen keel and vision to keep headed in the right direction.

It means that instead of measuring P31 or ourselves by what we're able to cram into a week, we need to take a long view of life and choose eyes to see way out to the horizon. There we see P31, whose rich and artful vistas reveal a woman who is not afraid to try new things. She is not defined by her roles; rather she is the re-creator of them. She is an imaginative cook, is good with money, and has the gift of closing a deal. She is a philanthropist, involved in her community, and an artist with a brilliant sense of style and humor. She creates healthy boundaries with her family and her work, and she is known as a wise and generous mentor. Suddenly this incredible woman of whom I have lived in hatred and disdain begins to look more and more like women I know and—even more surprisingly—like me.

Hidden between the lines in these passages, the true P31 drew from these same lessons in buoyancy. No doubt the secrets came hard and much the same way we learn them—in the moment. Somehow she learned to sequence her choices and roles during every season of her life—her fluid buoyancy act occurred over a number of years and at various stages of womanhood. Her life took many turns in the road. It reveals the story of a woman who knew that mothers fill more than a single role and that all women's work has integrity and value. It is a perspective that helps mothers like me feel empowered.

In Proverbs God sketches her quickly, like an artist who is only beginning a great work. We are left with an impression of who she was. She was never finished so that our hearts and imaginations could complete the canvas, each adding the details of our own life to hers. P31 is a living work God is crafting inside us all.

P31 calls to me now from the side of the road, "Stop struggling and start living!" She tells me to laugh at the things that would tear me off my point of center—because my future is secure. My portrait is in process. Every day God adds a stroke as he fleshes out my impression, the legacy and life that I will leave behind. Some days I can see the picture clearly, but other days it seems obscured. On those days I need to review the frame of womanhood that God laid down long ago. It keeps me honest. It inspires me to keep sailing into the winds and storms of my everyday life.

Behind the unfinished work of Proverbs 31 are the lives of many incredible women: women who defied gravity, exceeded expectations, broke down boundaries, and remained true to their hearts. I often feel their prayers and sense that the path worn smooth by their lives lifts me. These women remind me, in the midst of insurmountable odds and pressure, that my keel will keep me buoyant and my heading is dead on. They shout to me from the sidelines that no matter what, somehow, miraculously, and even when I don't believe it, I will float.

2

DEEP WATERS

Lessons in Value

She is worth . . . more

He reached down from heaven and rescued me; he drew me out of deep waters.

PSALM 18:16 NLT

CRATER LAKE IS the seventh-deepest lake in the world. Its depths can only be measured by sonar. The trip to the bottom is 1,947 feet; there the sand is covered with lava blocks 650 feet long, left by calderas that collapsed millions of years ago. Nothing prepares you for the deep azure blue of the water or the lake's immense circumference. Visitors audibly, visibly gasp. This lake looks so wide and so deep, you feel you're in the midst of a mystery, where all the answers may never be entirely clear.

Motherhood took me to the bottom of Crater Lake with one of those 650-foot rocks tied around my waist.

When my husband, Pat, and I went to bring Patrick and Andrea home to us, we had only been married nine months. I panicked because I had no time to get used to the idea, no time to count the costs, even if I had known what they were.

It was just as well. I became a mother the way some people win cars. The attorney handed me the keys and said, "You are now the proud mother of two teenagers." The judge smiled at me and wished, "Good luck." I thanked them both, smiled back, and thought, *I love these children. I love my husband. I know they love me. How hard can anything be when you have love?*

I know now that's like telling yourself at the Indy 500 starting line to just put the key in the ignition and turn. It wasn't too long before I realized that I needed an operating manual for moms and I was running out of gas. But back then I was cooking endless meals and washing countless loads of laundry. I never stopped or sat down, it seemed, until my head hit the pillow. Everywhere I stepped, something needed my attention—needed me. My insides ached with a longing for something I could not name. I had somehow spun off center like a poor, overworked washer, and the rocking was making me angry. My resentment turned to panic. I felt like motherhood was taking me down, deeper and deeper, and the bottom still wasn't in sight. I was tied up with anger and frustrated over the tightening ropes crafted by my own hands. Before I knew it, I found myself looking for light above, praying that God would find me and help me resurface.

Instead I just kept seeing murky waters.

I honestly thought I was alone, that what I felt was probably the product of my own neurosis and selfish sin. *Maybe I'm not motherhood material,* I thought. *Maybe I just haven't given enough of myself—my whole self—over to God. Maybe I've deluded myself that I can do this.* The doubts mounted the longer I waited for that feeling of calling to kick in—the one everyone told me moms experience.

I am still waiting.

Somewhere along this road of motherhood, the real me was in jeopardy of being replaced by a selfless, placid plow horse. I feared losing myself. I began to question too: *Why am I doing this? Who really cares if my floor is dirty and the top of my washer is stacked to the ceiling with clothes? How did I become head chump in charge of the meaningless housework? Is this all there is—housework and selflessly serving kids who won't realize all that's done for them until they're twenty-five? What about my aspirations, my dreams?*

So when I recall how someone once said to me, "What an amazing thing you have done for your kids—you saved them," I know a confession is due. It would be wonderful if that were true, but we all know it isn't. I didn't save my kids. Not even the best mother could do that.

The truer statement is that God saved *me* with motherhood. He gave me a glimpse of what I could be and how much he wanted me—and he wanted me to get a good look from my knees.

Why couldn't you have made me like P31? I've prayed. *How can I be a better wife and mother—and enjoy it?*

My own questions made me speak out loud, even at the risk of committing what might very well be a form of mommy treason. I sought out other mothers and asked if they really liked their jobs. I asked, "Do you feel on top of your game? How do you care for your kids' hearts and souls? How do you practice your gifts and talents and art in the middle of the cooking, cleaning, taxi duty, and family counseling demands of every day?" I didn't care if these were the questions we all feared. I had to know.

What I found was many other wives, moms, and women who felt they too were being swallowed up by some vast expanse of duty like endlessly deep waters. They too felt their clarity of heart and sense of self were lost somewhere down at the bottom.

30

No one seemed quite sure what to do about it.

There was the tried-but-untrue idea that motherhood, and becoming Proverbs-31-like, is simply a balancing act. The implication was that if you used your time wisely, joined the right mothering group, employed the right cleaning products, and followed the right parenting guidelines, then balance could be possible.

But no one really gets to find balance in this act. Only Jesus could step with just the right weight on his toes and heels to walk on water.

P31 must have known the simpler, more freeing thing I'm now learning: God wants to help us find buoyancy. He wants us to know and live in the knowledge of our value in the middle of a lake of chaos, at the bottom of the teeth-grinding experience of motherhood. God wants to make us resilient with the light of conviction that whatever our job is, our worth has already been established. It is not in what we do but who we are.

The reason we need this kind of buoyancy is that motherhood has many inherent traps. The traps have been set across time and cultures. They were not set in malice, but through self-protection and fear. Motherhood carries propaganda of all sizes and weights. Some of the propaganda tells us that motherhood is a selfless act, and if you can't cut it, well, you just aren't mommy material. Some would say that anyone who expects praise from her kids probably shouldn't be a mother. True, kids are selfish, and to even start the engine on motherhood, you must first have shown some aptitude for heroic behavior.

My sister Cindee is the kind of mother who gives selflessly and generously without blinking. I've never heard her say she thought anything was unfair or that she was tortured over the thankless inequity of the housework or emotional investment. Still, I think we all want to feel that our work is valued, that our dreams and prayers carry more weight in God's eyes than clean floors or perfectly balanced dinners.

Then I think back on my own childhood and ask myself, Who made all those packed lunches that mysteriously appeared every morning? Who came to my defense when I almost flunked first grade? Who sewed all my Barbie clothes and made every birthday cake?

It was, of course, my mother.

If I were to ask my mother how she handled being invisible, being taken for granted as she practiced all her heroic acts of kindness, she would no doubt smile and tell me that the reward will come later and one day my kids will remember all my heroic acts as well.

Delayed gratification has never been my strong suit. I often think about the quote "The hand that rocks the cradle rules the world." This may sound good on paper, but frankly, after my turn at rocking, I've never felt less powerful.

Statistics show that stay-at-home mothers have their lack of worth and power confirmed from several angles. We lose on taxes, Social Security, and wages that add up to an average loss of one million dollars. We miss out on promotions and bonuses, travel and extended education, and when other people ask us what we do, we must fish every time for a great-sounding spin on the most unappreciated position since the beginning of time.

Tell me again how we have clout?

The need to feel significant is both human and spiritual. As the psychologist Abraham Maslow explained in his theory on the hierarchy of needs, once our basic needs are met, other deeper needs surface, such as the needs for personal value, recognition, and stimulation.

Where does a mother go to feel amazing?

Mommy groups affirm us as good mothers when we stay home, and returning to work outside the home affirms us as something more than a mother. Could it be some of the good places we go may affirm us for all the wrong reasons?

I'm looking for God's affirmation, his view—not a binocular vantage point but an up-close and personal kind of explanation of how he wants me to travel. I don't want to cling to motherhood or any job like a life preserver and somehow expect it to keep me safe.

I remember the first time I took Andrea into the design firm I freelance for and showed her a book I helped design.

"Wow, you did this?" she said incredulously. It was as if she had made a major discovery that I could do something other than mop floors and make macaroni and cheese.

The owner of the firm said, "I bet you had no idea your mother could do that." This might be one of the freakiest aspects of being a mother: Your biggest audience doesn't have a clue who you really are—not really. It may be that very facet that makes us begin to question that ourselves.

The experts often deal with this extreme need to feel valued and purposeful by giving us suggestions to do more: volunteer at a hospital, invite the other stay-at-home mothers over for a lunch on your deck, walk farther, swim more laps, learn a new folk dance, visit the library, or take a computer course. In other words, fill your day up so that you won't realize that the ache inside you is getting bigger—instead of waiting for the truth to arrive deep in your gut. I just don't find any Scriptures that recommend that I deal with my depths by taking a scrapbooking class.

The desire to be valued is the breeding ground for all forms of perfectionism, which in itself is a form of religion that says if you are perfect, if you are good enough, then you will *be* enough.

I have friends who cannot walk away from a dirty kitchen, even if they are guests there. They work tirelessly to decorate and accessorize every corner of their homes. Their recipes are organized, they can produce their children's third grade report cards if asked, and their kids' bedrooms are creative masterpieces with matching paint, bedspreads, curtains, and tag boards with coordinating push pins.

I've tried this in part. A year ago I told Andrea we would decorate her room. When I took her to pick a paint color, she chose a vivid blue—the kind of blue that is hard to paint over, hard to cover. She then chose a star and moon motif in yellows and more shades of blue. The pieces and shades reminded me of Van Gogh's *Starry Night*. I asked Andrea several times if she thought her plan was a bit too much blue.

"No," she kept saying. "I love it."

So I ordered the bed-in-a-bag with moons and stars. I painstakingly painted her walls and ordered a border that would match. When I was finished, it was like standing inside a giant blueberry.

That evening she yelled at me and told me to stay out of her life. She reviewed her rights in detail. She told me that she was old enough to go to bed later, color her bangs green, shave her head, and get her driver's permit. She had already forgotten how I poured my heart out in blueberry love.

My efforts had become invisible.

Later that night she would cry for the biological mother she has not seen for years, the one she cries for beneath her blue, blue sky where only the clock ticks out the minutes. In her story I am the stand-in mom, the woman who was willing to paint her room, never realizing how hard it would be on my heart and my value to never feel like enough.

That is the problem with trying to be the perfect mom—the one portrayed in TV shows and commercials, the one smiling up from the pages of bed-in-a-bag catalogs. In reality none of our efforts is ever going to be enough.

Every mother feels unappreciated and invisible at some time in parenting, regardless of her heroic efforts. It's part of the trap that God wants us to exchange for the idea that our worth has already been established. It's why he had the description of P31 put down for us to study and write on our hearts—a description bracketed by this important promise from him especially to you: I know exactly what you are made of; I knit you in your mother's womb; you are fearfully and wonderfully made; I have weighed your worth and consider it rare and priceless; you are the jewel of great price; you have a purpose (see Ps. 139:13–14; Prov. 31:10).

These are words God has carved in wood and stone, written in calligraphy on papyrus and silk; they are the words that rescue the lives of women like me. He is the hero of these passages and my life; he tells me I am in a place of new beginnings and reinvention, reclaiming a place of distinction.

The woman of Proverbs 31 knew this down to her core. She reveled in her worth and in the praise of her community, her children, and her husband. She was clothed with strength and dignity; she could laugh at the days to come. Greater still, she knew in her gut that it was not the work of her hands, her status in the community, or her parenting skills that rescued her. It was her willingness to wait for God to uncover and reveal her worth over a lifetime.

This picture of a woman's value gives me hope that there will be other chapters, that while none of us is ever really aware of what we are capable of, God knows just how amazing we are.

My own perspective on motherhood often challenges God's promise that he values me as a gem with no equal. Motherhood has taken me to the end of myself, to the bottom, but at the same time it has eternally tied me to a larger and more extravagant story of God's love for me—a story that ultimately brings all eyes to God, who is so big I can't quite ever get my arms around him and yet so close that he keeps track of each tear I cry.

The lessons of motherhood teach me that in deep waters I may need to ask myself some hard questions about who I am, what my value is, and where I find my worth—really.

I believe with all my being that what is happening now to my interior story is critical to my resurfacing and to my buoyancy. It doesn't matter how deep we are or how long we wait. When God's big hand reaches down and pulls us out of the thick, murky waters, we will sparkle like a gem made under pressure and time, created with great care.

This is not all there is, not by a long shot.

3

BREATHING

Lessons in Letting Go

She speaks with wisdom

He himself gives life and breath to everything, and he satisfies every need there is.

ACTS 17:25 NLT

When I was seven my mother fell asleep at the wheel of our blue 1965 Volkswagen. We rolled through a farmer's fence, rolling six more times before thundering to a stop. Upon that final landing our Bug looked like it had been through a trash compactor. My father pulled each one of us from the wreckage, then flagged down an RV driver who helped us into his rig and drove us to the hospital.

On that cold Montana morning I learned that life was not linear. It was my first glimpse of the reality that we are not the ones holding the controls and life is both a gift and a mystery. Like that cloud of breath that passes our lips and hangs in the cold morning air, life reorganizes our priorities and our feeling of control vanishes, dissipating bit by bit, particle by particle, floating out and away as mysteriously as it appeared.

Breathing is more than taking in oxygen. It's an attitude—an attitude of acceptance that our journey was never supposed to be linear and we were never supposed to travel a predictable route. I will have to fight to stay free of my great need to have life the way I want it.

Between my first breath as God's daughter after baptism in the icy waters of Lake Washington and my last gasp on earth, my path will be as free-form as our '65 Volkswagen rolling through that field. It is critical that I remember to breathe, remember that regardless of the state of my kids, my husband, or my floors, life with God is a road trip with detours and dead ends and sometimes even crashes along the way.

For some women this may be no issue, but I am a recovering control freak. I'm not the kind to fuss over clean ovens, but I paw the ground like a rabid animal when it comes to the right art for a book cover or just the right shade of paint for my walls. My kids scatter the other way when the paint chips surface.

I visibly twitch in front of the hair color section at the drugstore, where all the women smile at me from the front of the boxes as I strain toward my goal of finding the perfect shade of red that won't make my head glow in the dark.

When I entertain, I like a spread, but I wince when my kids insist that celery stuffed with cheese is an appetizer. The perfume I wear can only be purchased in Italy, which complicates my husband's life immeasurably, and don't even get me started about coffee, because I will confess I'm a java snob.

How crazy is it when I take anything to this level of perfectionism? How messed up am I that I cannot let go of behaviors that don't serve God but are there to glorify myself? Doesn't God know P31 is part of my problem—how I measure myself against her and always feel I come up short? Does he see how I wrestle with the line between doing my best and choosing the best?

Yesterday, on Memorial Day, my husband rolled out his industrial smoker and fired it up at 8:00 A.M. He proceeded to smoke fifteen racks of ribs and four chickens, and we fed family and friends.

This morning when I got up to make coffee, my feet were sticking to the floor, dishes were still in the sink, the garbage can was full, and barbeque sauce was splattered on several cupboards.

I surveyed the damage with a practiced gaze. My left eye started to twitch as I reached for the coffee grinder with one hand and my favorite French roast with the other. I poured coffee beans into the grinder, capped the lid, and leaned on the start button as the blades released that perfumed aroma. *Maybe,* I had the fleeting thought, *I could blow up the kitchen and just start over.*

In days past such a setting would have ruined my morning. Now I make the coffee, breathe deep, and anticipate a bite of leftover barbeque. I remember the appreciative smiles of our friends, the magic of a great meal, and the joy of having a husband who comes alive behind an apron and a good barbeque rub. It's a simple thing—breathing. The floor will get cleaned, the dishes washed, and the sauce removed from my cupboards, but the memories of barbeque days and friends will be with us forever.

We need to be able to let go and breathe when our universe gets small and airless. It's too easy to try to control small, unimportant things. But with a deep breath we can stop, think, and get a bigger view of the world. Without it we can feel ourselves twisting into something we loathe.

This exercise works for me: When the urge to control leaves me gasping, I ask myself a series of questions. Is this my job or is it God's? Is this crazy-making or is it profitable? Will this give my kids positive memories of their time with me, or will they think I'm a shrew with no life? Will I like myself at the end of the road—and will God?

From an artistic view, breathing in could be called inspiration. If I don't take time to breathe, I will miss what it is God wants me to see along the way, his inspiration. More importantly, I am sure to make myself crazy in the process. I desperately need to experience the space between breathing in and breathing out.

Sometimes I gasp, "God, help me to let go so I won't become the woman and mother of my nightmares. Help me to disengage so I can stay in the game and on the road." My hope is that God has enough oxygen and that the instructions he has given us will finally convince me that I cannot carry the load myself.

The emotional rub comes from thinking I'm a domestic diva who, like Mary Poppins, can pull magic from my big bag of tricks. I think I can fix anything—my kids, my husband, my home—whip up a dynamite meal, and add on a fabulously decorated guest room before lunch. Yes, I can make magic happen . . . for maybe a day. Maybe.

I can't stay in this mode long before I realize I am way out there and I need to breathe. The pull on me to be a super-achiever is enormous because my insides lie. They tell me my worth is in what I can do, who I can save. Just being isn't enough.

I know I'm not alone; I see supermoms sweating over things that just aren't that important every day. When I find myself yelling at my son because his room smells like something died in it, a voice inside me gently prods, "Let's review, shall we? Is this all that's important? Can't you close the door?"

I like to carry a picture of God's living room window in my head. I see it as a huge one with a panoramic view. I imagine that the view from the inside out shows me in his garden, pawing the ground, trying to plant something the right way while all around me are tomatoes as big as my head and morning glories hanging heavy on their branches. I'm in a garden that is already magnificent trying to plant something that is miniscule in comparison.

The breathing test in my own life starts with giving up my right to be right. There are a lot of times I may be right, but maybe there is choice I haven't considered.

Two weeks ago my daughter shaved the back of her head and colored it pink. Will my opinions build her esteem? When my husband bought a 2003 Goldwing motorcycle, even though I didn't think it was the best idea and I might have been right, did my opinion help? Breathing begins with closing my mouth and choosing my battles. In God's big picture, being right isn't really my job.

In order to keep our focus on building relationships and experiences with eternal value, we need to look for creative ways to carefully hold our opinions. When my son turned eighteen, I realized he had stopped listening to me. It happens. At eighteen, I stopped listening to my parents too. It wasn't until I was thirty that I found I could hear them again.

Of course what I felt Patrick needed to hear from me was quite the opposite of whatever my parents had wanted me to know. Yes, he needed to listen to me—this time was critical. *How is he ever going to get his act together when he doesn't get up until 10:30 every morning? Why doesn't he do something with his hair? Has he turned in all his forms for college? Is he really looking for a job, or is he spending all his time in music stores?*

It took me some time before I realized my questions could have been put to a brick with as much response as I could expect. In his heart and head, Patrick wasn't listening. He was already gone, ready to get on with his life, ready to make his own way. I had to let him go.

I wanted my departing words to be not those of a nagging mother but those of an enthusiastic fan. I got a blank book and I wrote down in it everything I would say if he were listening—in case he should ever ask. *Maybe when he is thirty,* I thought.

When Patrick came to live with us, we bought him an electric guitar, a Jackson. It had elegant lines wrapped in black lacquer with mother-of-pearl frets. It was a beauty.

I remember standing in the shop with his father, trying to decide whether we could afford it. We had already started to dream of what Patrick would play on it, and every time we made a payment, we dreamed a little more. It was like visiting a little piece of his destiny.

The day before Patrick's graduation from high school, he stood in the door to his room playing me a song he had written. Suddenly I looked down at his guitar and in horror realized he had used my sander to wear away the black lacquer edges, and he'd covered the pearl frets with ugly green tape.

He must have heard me take in air, because he stopped. "What?" he said, already knowing, then, "I think it looks cool."

I was suppressing an aneurysm. Just when the blood was about to explode in my head and, admittedly, after thinking several phrases I won't repeat, I heard a voice in my head whisper, *Just breathe.* I stood back looking at Patrick. Whose guitar was it? Who did this hurt anyway? I didn't say the things I was tempted to and simply took a deep breath, closed the door, and walked away.

The next day I watched Patrick receive his diploma, then watched him play his upright bass until the sweat rolled down his face. The music came from deep in his gut. I could feel his passion vibrating down the strings. Wearing the suit we had bought him for formal gigs, he was concentrating so hard that his eyebrows touched. It was like watching someone fly, and all we could do was stand in awe of it.

Last year for Christmas I found Patrick an old army trunk and painted it. Printed on the top is IF YOU CAN PLAY, YOU WON'T STARVE. On the sides it reads THIS WAY TO THE ROAD LESS TRAVELED. I believe that it is his road, and I'm simply glad that I was part of it and most of all that I choose daily to live in a world big enough to take it all in.

Life with God means I am also on the road less traveled, even if some days I refuse to believe it. When I was seven and my family would take achingly long car trips to do errands, I would repeatedly whine, "Where are we going?"

My mother would calmly reply, "Crazy."

This used to send me into a complete and utter head-splitting spin. I mean, when you're seven, where do you go with that?

Forty years later, it's crystal clear. Being a parent is a kind of quirky sanity test. Most of us fail; the ones who seem unscathed just aren't right in the head. I have come to the conclusion that kids are nonlinear beings that are supposed to make us crazy. They are part of our uncharted territory, the road less traveled, and no matter where we steer, God seeks to loosen our grip on the wheel.

There are days I feel I'm living in an asylum. I know there are other places where healthier and certainly more mature moms are having conversations with their kids that never end with slammed doors and gnashing of teeth, but I do not know them. I am grateful for that. I thought I knew a lot about parenting, but the truth is that what I knew could have left room in a shoe box.

If you were to ask my kids about my early days of motherhood they could tell you some stories that would end with phrases like "whacked out" or "control freak." I will admit to it all, because one thing they have taught me is that I don't have to do anything to be significant to them. If I sit long enough in one place, they will both find me, sometimes one on either side. There will be tickling and teasing and lots of hugs. They are teaching me that what is important is not whether I can save them or how clean my house is but rather that I am present, conscious, and breathing.

On the road to buoyancy are lessons in breathing and how it gives you time to focus on what God is doing. P31 must have discovered that God's purposes would be made known to her if she would just take time to breathe. The pause, the very act, gave her time to seek him so that her words would be sweet and her counsel wise.

God knew her details. He ordered her day, and she allowed him to interrupt her. She knew it was his hand that nudged her toward the side of the road or down a path less worn. He was the shift of the wind, the change of the tides, and the fullness of the moon. She found him in the place where small changes made her restless, the final straw that made her slow down. She knew that God didn't just show up when she cried out for him—he was concerned with her every breath. I believe she relinquished her right to be right, to be perfect, and to be enough. She kept her eyes always on the significance of her steps and their eternal value.

I'm learning that life is not linear. My buoyancy will depend on how I choose to travel. I need to let go of all the things in my life that aren't that important and give control over to God. He never promised that our lives will unfold neatly before us. He promises to give us a bigger world so that his purposes can be established, to give us inspiration to breathe in and the welcome relief of breathing out. He promises to give us air.

4

LAP SWIM

Lessons in Judging

Give her the rewards

Do not throw the arrow which will return against you.

KURDISH PROVERB

THE GIRLS SLIDE gracefully down their aquamarine lanes: down, under, then up, forward, down, under, up. Andrea slips through her channel like a mermaid, weightless but finding some rhythm. I watch my daughter change before me with each stroke. She's in that strange and awesome place of evolving where the awkwardness and timidity of her youth begins to submit to an emerging individual poise and uniqueness.

Today as I watch her, I wonder if she can sense what makes her exquisite. Like most young girls her age, she judges herself by the airbrushed expectations of what advertisers call *beauty* and the cool girls call *hot*. Girls her age convince themselves they need cosmetic surgery because of the comparisons and the unattainable perfection of pop stars frozen on magazine covers and in videos and movies—the images that take herds of stylists and many edits to make. Although I've done everything I can to convince my daughter that she was made to be unique, she just rolls her eyes and points out that she seriously doubts I ever went to high school.

I know that look. I understand that feeling.

"What do you do?" a woman asked me once. She was lean, with steel gray eyes and a high-definition body, and she sized me up like an athlete.

"I'm a wife and a mom," I replied. "I have two kids, a house, and a husband."

"No," she insisted. "I mean what do you do?"

I repeated that my hands were full with domestic duties and the administration of my family.

She cocked her head to one side like small dogs do when they aren't sure where you threw the ball. I immediately knew what was coming next. It is times like these that I realize I have an enemy. She wore a dress and pretty shoes with heels instead of jeans and socks that matched (maybe). She wasn't picking up on the stay-at-home-mommy lingo; she had another agenda.

"What do you do for a job?" she asked.

My mind raced for the right spin on my domestic duties. "My daughter has some problems," I blurted, hoping this woman would see that I was clearly a saint. The minute it left my mouth, I knew it was a huge mistake, like walking out of the restaurant bathroom and not realizing the end of the toilet paper roll has somehow stuck to your heel.

It took me a moment to realize I was mad—the kind of anger that comes when you feel you've just been torn into by one of your own pack.

I looked around. I wasn't alone. There were a whole lot of other women standing next to me.

Somewhere in the process of growing up, we all deal with judgments and comparisons. Our greatest obstacle to unearthing our own uniqueness is the judgment we place on ourselves and the perceived comparisons by our peers. We aren't really looking for that one thing that sets us apart and makes us dazzling. We just want to fit in and play it safe.

51

Let's face it: Sometimes it's just easier to hide behind roles, groups, and committees. It's as if we are magnetized to huddle in the comfort of being part of a crowd. There's safety in numbers, and when the world judges us, some common denominator somehow softens the blow.

When I became a mom, I got lots of feedback from well-meaning people. Pastors told me "a mother's primary job is to be home for those kids," and other church members described it with words like *calling* and *vocation*. Even my mother, who worked most of my life, agreed.

I felt a lot of pressure to choose a mommy pack or group as I simultaneously became acclimated to the role.

Those of us who come into motherhood later in life have the benefit of perspective. Many of us have held fulfilling jobs that we didn't mind staying up into the wee hours to do or being stretched to the limits to finish.

To say that motherhood is suddenly my true vocation doesn't really make a lot of sense to me. Admittedly, I look at this motherhood experience differently than most, and anytime we find ourselves in a new role in life, we search our memory banks for what helped us find our way through opinions and judgments in the past.

Still, you know that saying "When mommy's not happy, nobody's happy"? Guess what happens when a whole lot of mommies aren't happy? The Working and Stay-at-Home Mommy Camps are divided, and they have plenty of angst and comparisons between them. The comparisons range from public school versus home schooling to working outside the home versus exclusively inside it, from day care versus do-it-yourself to breast feeding versus bottle, and bonding—let's not even get started on that topic. Wherever there are different perspectives, there is judgment, and judgment always comes from a place God begs us not to go: "Stop judging others, and you will not be judged," Jesus said. "Stop criticizing others, or it will all come back on you" (Luke 6:37 NLT). My early struggles at being a stay-at-home mother were exacerbated by the judgments that came from those who wanted to tag me, name me, and classify me and my kids.

"Your son is in high school, right?" an acquaintance inquired. Before I could answer she blurted, "My daughter just made the track team and has just been accepted into the Honor Society. We are so excited that she is doing so well. She has a 3.5—no, I think it's a 3.6. Anyway, she is applying for every scholarship she can get her hands on. It's just amazing. She hardly tries at all. I mean, she is just a natural brainiac, and she is doing a mission trip to Mexico this year with her youth group, and. . . ."

I smiled a plastic smile and kept watching to see if she was breathing.

"Sooooo," she finally concluded, "how is your son doing?"

"Well," I hesitated, but only for a second, "he's over there." I pointed to the boy dressed all in black with pants that looked like wild animals had attacked the hems.

"Oh?" she managed to squeak.

"Yes, he is quite the artist and a musician, and he has a 2.5 average." I didn't tell her that was a vast improvement from the straight F average from the year before.

"Oh," she squeaked again.

Should I continue? I wondered. My son is amazing, but the comparisons to her daughter were not going to put him on equal ground. I really wanted to tell her that Patrick does amazing impersonations that make me laugh until my sides hurt, that he is a wonderful son who often rubs my shoulders and takes great interest in my day, that he is a compassionate person and loves people—and does it count that he is the only other person in the family (besides me) who likes sci-fi movies?

"Does he have learning disabilities?" she inquired.

"No." I suppressed the urge to screw her head on tighter. "But he does have an IQ of 167."

She chattered on about how IQ is really the important thing, after all, and her daughter. . . .

I felt a little like I was playing Jeopardy and the other mother had chosen all the categories. How many of us mothers would be in the final round if the category were THIGHS THAT ARE CELLULITE-FREE?

Do I wish my son had a 3.6? Clearly it would be better for him. Yet is it something I want to define him? No.

Sometimes God uses our kids to bring us back to earth and help us remember that we are not apples and we can't be compared to one another.

I came into motherhood expecting opposition. I had to fight for my kids in court. I stood in front of a judge and miraculously convinced him that I was fit to mother two teenagers. Make no mistake, when it came to my kids, I was ready to wrestle an alligator. I just wasn't expecting those alligators to be other women and mothers.

Our enemy doesn't want us to grow up. He wants us to stay dependent on people and their opinions because, frankly, they are his secret weapon. People can tear us up with their comparisons and their judgments. His ultimate goal is to have us give up before we begin. He wants us to live without a sense of our own compass so that he can trap us with the words of our judges.

Our judges are everywhere. Women compare. We judge. We are quick to size each other up. What does she do? What is she wearing? Who is she married to? How much does she make? What kind of mom is she? What does she do, really? We quickly position others and therefore ourselves in the pack.

I'm guilty. I've done it. I remember being in my twenties and wondering what stay-at-home moms did. *What could possibly fill up an entire day at home?* It baffled me. Now that I know, I find myself struggling not to judge women who judge.

If you watch animal packs, you can get a clue as to some human pack dynamics. The pack mentality is both inclusive and exclusive. It judges and restricts. It is one-dimensional living, and there are only two roles in a pack: one leader and many followers. In wolf packs, the dominant alpha female is in charge. Less dominant wolves hold their tails down and often lower their bodies. To show that they accept the alpha wolf's authority, the less dominant wolves roll over on their backs, exposing their underbellies. The dominant wolf stands over the followers. These dominance rules keep the wolves in a pack from fighting among themselves and hurting each other—they make life manageable.

We have an inner drive that says to file away or box up those we aren't comfortable with; we do this to make life more manageable. Once we tag others, we feel better and can move on. We feel like we have control. Most of us have managed our lives in this way at one time or another. When someone hurts us, we need to establish that they have some deep and complex problem. When someone makes us angry, we conclude they are bad or malicious. When someone makes us uncomfortable or we don't think we have anything in common with them, we conclude that they're boring and would most likely find us intimidating. We even censor ourselves at times to fit in and to seek out other like-minded women—women who think like us, believe like us, mother like us. We want to be affirmed by them. What's wrong with that?

Maybe nothing . . . except that God never meant us to roll over to be accepted in a pack. He wants us to make our life choices even when the pack does not affirm them. And while he knows we need friends and soul mates, he doesn't want us trapped by them.

Women are more than a single role, more than a single career. We are unique beings who should never be compared. We need to model this to our daughters so that they will never let something made so precious by God be judged or restricted. If we allow ourselves to live in others' judgments, we will be severely disappointed at the end of our lives.

One of my favorite movies is *The Unsinkable Molly Brown*. It is an incredibly cheesy musical about oil heiress Molly Brown, who breaks into Denver society from a humble background. Played by Debbie Reynolds, Molly is a scrappy optimist who refuses to be put down by all the "highfalutin hobbitynobs" of the upscale neighborhood.

I've always identified with her. The feeling she experienced of coming up from behind is such a powerful one for me. It grabs me by the jugular and makes me want to spit on the floor and walk like I just got off a horse. Most of all, it makes me want to tell all those who don't believe in me, "Watch out Denver, 'cause here I come, and I'm coming to stay."

So, to the next woman who asks me what I do, really—I *am*, really.

It's taken me time to get my footing, but I got it finally, and I "ain't taking any of your messed-up thinking to heart."

God is for every woman who unselfishly delays her dreams and every woman who worries that she is selfish in the pursuit of them. I am rooting for all of us that one day we all will "get it," and our reason for existence will not be justified by how much we can do or where we fit in the pack.

Until then I will stick with Molly, who was a real Proverbs 31 woman. She would say that "a wise woman builds her house, but a foolish woman tears hers down with her own hands" (Prov. 14:1 NLT). Then she would add, "Do I need to paint ya a picture? We can't afford to judge. In doing so, we tear down ourselves with our bare hands. When we feel justified in judging, something has got to rise up inside us and get real."

I believe there's a little Molly in us all, and if we build each other up, God promises that he will not only give us buoyancy but also make us unsinkable.

P31 shows us that the key to motherhood is who is at the center of our universe and whether we can make our choices free of judgment. She knew that titles didn't impress God. God didn't care whether she was a CEO or a mom in jeans and flip-flops. He wanted her heart. He made her for a purpose, so that the value of her life would bring all eyes back to him. He wanted every part of her to vibrate with the knowledge that there was greatness in her and that she would be rewarded for not just her deeds but for all she was and would become. He wove her individuality into her depths. She is the standard that we aspire to. She would say a woman of incomparable quality is a piece of art, which with age becomes more significant as the colors deepen, becoming rich and multifaceted. This can only happen when hands do not hesitate but rather understand what they were created for and by whom.

I'm still working on it. Some days I desperately want to compare, want to judge, want to find my pack, because I think that would solve all my problems. But in this buoyancy act there are more days now that I am standing on my own and swimming in a lane by myself. I stand wet and cold in a Speedo with water dripping down my face. Deep down I'm not fooling myself—there will be days that are miserable. But there will also be days when I am swimming in my channel, weightless, each stroke finding its rhythm, and it is then that I can see what makes me undeniably dazzling.

5

TREASURE

Lessons in Happiness

Her lamp does not go out

If you never did,
You should.
These things are fun,
And fun is good.

Dr. Seuss, *One Fish, Two Fish, Red Fish, Blue Fish*

When I was nine, my family moved to a house on Lake Whatcom, Washington. Our two-story house was small and set back on a narrow lot that sloped down to the lake. Our attic bedrooms had lots of cubbyholes. I particularly loved the summers there. My sister and I would get up early to fish with Dad in a little twelve-foot aluminum boat that smelled of gasoline and bait.

We sat on the glassy water patiently waiting for a fish, looking down into the dark green depths for anything that might stir beneath the surface. In the afternoons we dove for treasure at the bottom of the lake—all the way down, touching the bottom. We never tired of this and recovered rocks and pieces of wood like they were valuable secret jewels and lost booty. In our imaginations, seeking and recovering treasure was serious business as we laughed in the sun, buoyant and youthful. We never thought there might come a day we would think it otherwise.

Of course it did. So in my living room I have a large Montana river rock chiseled with these words: DANCE LIKE NO ONE IS WATCHING. The rock is a hefty reminder to play even though there will always be things that the world says are more important. I keep the rock because sometimes I feel guilty playing, embarrassed to be caught in the act, because play doesn't hold the same importance as painting the living room or retiling the bathroom.

What if I were to spend the whole day reading a book? What if I were to take off with my husband on our Goldwing and cycle down the coast and back up again just for the fun of it? What if I started taking belly dancing or tap dance? What if I just played games with my kids more often?

When we play we are children again, willing to take risks, unafraid of judgments and limitations. We were never intended to live all of life seriously. We were designed to play. Play is a limitless sphere where God teaches us over and over that we were made to celebrate his creation and to be awed by our own creativity.

Play has many different benefits. It makes us better problem solvers; it keeps us young; it helps us forget our worries; it rekindles our imaginations; and it keeps us from being boring adults. Most of us don't play enough, myself included. Any adult knows that on a daily basis there are lists of lists of things we need to accomplish—play is usually not one of them. The truth is, how well we play can touch many facets of our lives. In a culture that depends on creativity and innovation, play can be the difference between failure and success. How creative can you be if you are unwilling to or do not make time to explore your own playfulness? How innovative will your ideas be if you haven't tried something fun and new?

For the last twenty years I have had an agreement with myself that at least once a month I needed to get lost in a creative project. Exercising my creativity today is like the hours I spent as a child finger painting or the pottery projects I proudly modeled and brought home to my mother. I might paint a piece of furniture, craft some earrings, or make a ballet tutu for my favorite little ballerina. Silly? Maybe, but it helps me remember how to play. When I get lost in a project, I get reconnected to the treasure God has laid in my foundations. I also find youthful energy, because in the very act and process of play, it often suddenly dawns on us that we don't have to act our age.

Last night I played Scrabble with Patrick. I didn't play like a forty-seven-year-old woman with two cars and a mortgage. You can ask my son, who beat me with the one word *quailed* (I'd never heard of it, but upon a dictionary check learned it's a J. R. R. Tolkien kind of word that gets pulled out just for show). As we challenged each other's words, giggling and teasing each other, I realized I was no longer The Mom. I was the girl who crafted whole neighborhoods from Popsicle sticks and painted pot holders just for fun.

When I hear someone say, "Why doesn't she act her age?" I think, *Just maybe she gets it and you don't. Don't you understand that the fountain of youth resides in your head and the only way to release its powerful juice is to play?*

When I was twenty-two I met a woman who was and is ageless. I call her my other mother. She showed me what being creative and at play looked like. I was a college student looking for a place to live when Vivianna emerged from a doorway dressed in electric layers of color and earrings the size of laser discs. Standing six feet tall in her bare feet, she filled the room with the energy of a high-speed printing press. She extended long, heavily-ringed fingers to me and announced herself, "I'm Vivianna."

In the months to come I discovered that everything she touched became infused with her life, a deep faith, eternal optimism, and a profound sense of play. She evangelized daily, often bringing those she met home for dinner. On Thursdays she fasted. On Fridays the fragrance coming from her kitchen would make my mouth water. Her journals, filled with her conversations with God and shared openly, were written in a loopy scrawl with multicolored inks. Often in the morning I would hear her playing her ukulele. She was a painter, a calligrapher, and a dancer; she taught me Tahitian dances and gave me my first leather-bound journal. She was larger than life, and her very presence reached beyond her neat kitchen filled with shiny copper pots and fragrant figs out into the streets of her community. She was an artist-at-large in the world, and she taught me that being creative was not one single act but, with playfulness, the very act of living itself.

Too many folks live like play and imagination are things that we must outgrow—like they are not serious or real and we shouldn't expect to have fun in the workplace or church or as adults. This is one myth motherhood dispels, for in mothering we discover with our children how to play again. We see that there is a room in our hearts called PLAY where the rules are fluid and imagination reigns. This space is all about having fun, being a little crazy, and trying something new just to see what happens. It is a place close to God and very much about being in his presence whether that place is a river in Montana or a game of paintball in the backyard.

Today I watched my mother get lost in her watercolor paintings. She was having so much fun that occasionally she let out a squeal of delight. She is seventy and doesn't have one gray hair on her head, and neither of us could find a wrinkle until just last week. My mom bounced into this world, and she touches down occasionally just to show us how it's done.

Several months ago she joined the Red Hat Society, a group dedicated to providing fun for women. Every meeting is populated with red and pink hats in all sizes and styles worn by all sorts of members. Reminiscent of playing dress-up as a child, the Red Hat Society goes everywhere in full regalia. It began as a result of a few women deciding to greet middle age with verve, humor, and élan—women who believe in silliness as the comic relief of life. They know that adults especially need to play more, and so their mission is to join red-gloved hands and go for the gusto together. Underneath this frivolity the Red Hat Society says they share a bond of affection forged by common life experiences and a genuine enthusiasm for going wherever life takes them next.

When I heard about this group, a part of me thought, *Wow, I could get into that.* My enthusiasm was quickly extinguished by a kind of party-pooper, evil-queen attitude inside that reminded me that my responsibilities and job were serious. That's exactly why I know I need the Red Hat Society—because I need to play more and feel less guilty in the process.

64

I need to slow down enough to hear the possibilities and laugh enough to forget myself. I need to get silly enough to open up my problem-solving systems. I've seen that secret mom powers can come from a little play.

When the kids first moved in, I had to find a way to give them small, immediate rewards for doing a job properly. I got an idea from the school where I had enrolled Patrick for help with his math. I had noticed that there Patrick (who never did homework in school) was excited about learning and began completing his assignments. One day he came home with a game he told me he had purchased at the school reward store with tokens. The students earned tokens every day for finishing parts of their work; each kid put theirs in a jar with their name on it, like a bank. Every day the kids were allowed time to look in the store, and when they had enough tokens to get what they wanted, they could redeem them.

It was a brilliant idea, so I quickly patterned something after it for home. My kids were introduced to a new system known as The Fishbowl. As a reward for doing their household chores and taking a hand in keeping up our house, they could put their hand in a fishbowl and pull out a token. Some of the tokens said MISS ONE NIGHT OF DISHES or PICK A VIDEO AT THE MOVIE STORE or MAGAZINE OR BOOK OF YOUR CHOICE or, one of their favorites, $10 SHOPPING SPREE. They could also get CD tokens, and five would buy them a new CD. The kids loved The Fishbowl, and Pat and I did too.

In fact, I wonder now why we stopped using it. Did we fall into the world's thinking that our teenagers were too grown up?

Maybe, but these days I'm thinking maybe I need someone to let me pick from The Mommy Fishbowl. There would be tokens like ONE-HOUR MASSAGE, BUY A RED HAT, $100 SHOPPING SPREE, and NIGHT BY MYSELF AT THE BEACH. There would be tokens with points I could earn toward TWO WEEKS IN ITALY or A CABIN FOR THE SUMMER.

I can dream, can't I?

Organizations and corporations have developed positions for people who are basically playground directors. Their jobs entail thinking up fun incentives and games to make people happier and their work more fun, and because of these factors, increase productivity.

I'm convinced that motherhood needs a playground director. Reinstating nap time followed by cookies and juice wouldn't be a bad idea either.

As I looked at camps for my daughter, I found myself thinking, *Why isn't there a summer camp for moms?* I would gratefully turn in my dish towel for a baseball glove and play. My memories of camp are not that great, mostly of fighting off mosquitoes and having to wear "outfits" sewn by my mom, with matching scarves that made me look like Heidi, while the other kids wore jeans. Still, today as I sit writing this book in my laundry room/office, trying to ignore the constant knocks on my door, the phone ringing, and the dog butting the door with her head, I think it would be nice to go where someone

else makes dinner—and everyone helps clean up. I'd like to eat
s'mores, tell ghost stories, and go to bed late. I'd like to play
with my friends until I'm too tired to remove my clothes and
sleep so hard that the pillow imprints my face. I'd like to skip
to breakfast and race to dinner. Yes, I would like to go to camp
to catch fireflies, stare up at the sky, and just be a girl.

All we have to do is look at the nature of God to understand
where this playfulness comes from. We see his dabbling in
color and light and feel his breath of excitement in the next
experiment and the next. Look at the anteater or baboon and
at animals, birds, and amphibians with bodies that camou-
flage or turn bright colors. Birds that nest and bears that seek
caves. God knows how to play—who do we think taught us?
Who put inside us the unique aspect of our own nature that
recognizes and is fueled by the power of play?

The power of play translates into a life that is fun. I imagine P31 was the Kate Spade of her time. Kate Spade creates
brightly colored handbags that remind women that deep
down they are girls who occasionally want to replace their
compartmentalized carry-all bag for one that just says "play."
Kate started her company on a whim, for the fun of it, and it
has translated into a very successful venture.

P31 was a craftswoman, an artisan who wove garments
and made quilts. I think it was her love for her art that later
translated into a successful business selling her ornate and
colorful belts. She loved to play with color and texture and
the way a design came together. Her light burned late into the
night as she got lost in the creative process. She is a reminder

to us that we need to consistently honor our sense of fun as the treasure of our youth. Keep playing, keep exploring, and keep experimenting in life.

P31 shows us that the secret of our youth resides in our minds, our imaginations, and our ability to communicate our passion to those around us. God invites us to look with more then just our eyes, to draw with more than our hands. We are an integral part of God's creative juices on this earth. We can't afford to forget to play, or we will miss the open door to the next idea or the bigger opportunity. In this way God calls us all to be artists, keen observers who capture the general impression of what he is up to and enter into it with our hearts open wide to the possibilities.

God wants us to ask "Why not?" He reminds us that "nothing will be impossible with God" (Luke 1:37). When we ask the questions we weren't afraid to ask as children, we find the answers are often hidden in the limitations we ourselves have accepted. In our operating instructions God calls us to be artists, to be creators, to dance like no one is watching. He made us to play like it's serious business and to guard against the day that we would think it otherwise.

6

SURFACING

Lessons in Real Beauty

Beauty is fleeting

Beautiful young people are accidents of nature,
But beautiful old people are works of art.

ELEANOR ROOSEVELT,
"I AM A BEAUTIFUL OLD PERSON"

THE SURFACE OF the water was marked by the occasional flip of a tail causing a water ring to radiate out in neat circles. Just below the surface, the picture changed completely; here was a different world where brightly colored gills breathed life in rapid movements and glided through the liquid that held them. Above and below the water—only a thin skin separated the two worlds. From above, the skin of the surface looked like an edge, a floor; from below, the skin looked like a container wall. The skin itself was a sort of gate from one dimension to the next. Below, where I spent the least time, was a complex and fascinating world God had made in secret.

Under my skin, I haven't always felt beautiful.

At forty-seven, I'm told by the advertising world that I'm on my way out. It's a time of adjustment, of flux, where I pause and look at what has changed and what still remains.

But God tells us everyone arrives beautiful, and in the process of time and life, he sets about to reveal all that he designed beneath our surface. He makes the way for us to break that skin of water, as if he takes us below the surface and plants the ideas: *You think you know what you're like? Look below the surface and see more, see the fearful and wonderful nature of this creation. Think about the awesome plan to expose your true beauty.*

The great artists always look beneath the surface. Michelangelo would ponder a rock for days, weeks, even months because he believed that by really looking one could finally see the figure trapped inside the rock. He believed that the rock would show him what beauty lay beneath its surfaces. Only then, when the rock "spoke," would he begin to carve; he chiseled away what was unnecessary and kept what was essential.

All artists know that creation is a process of elimination and refinement; the best design solution is simple and clean; the best sculptures can be viewed from multiple angles. Yet women, including myself, often obsess over our one-dimensional surfaces, valuing our containers and disregarding the real masterpiece in process beneath our surface.

God's view of beauty is good news for women like me because it tells us that while our surfaces change, real beauty is our unique gift, our something quirky. It says that on those days that we feel the ebb of youth leaving our shores, we can count on the fact that what makes us glimmer will always be with us.

The obsession over our surfaces is everywhere we look. This last week I counted eleven news stories on weight, hair loss, cosmetic surgery, and Botox injections. *Extreme Makeover*, a popular television show, follows people willing to go through multiple painful procedures to be remade. I keep thinking that although I know this gives them a new confidence, there is something inherently wrong with altering yourself in extreme ways. God made us all differently—some of us he made with hips that could deliver a dump truck, noses the size of door knockers, and ears that flap in a breeze. What's not beautiful about that?

These shows and others add to the already colossal battle of women lacking self-confidence. We forget that our least favorite features are part of an individuality that God tells us is beautiful.

Yesterday my daughter told me that as soon as she has a job she is going to start saving for cosmetic surgery. I found myself wanting to shout, "What's up with that?" Andrea is a very pretty girl. People often remark on her blue eyes, blonde hair, and gorgeous smile. But instead of screaming, I asked why. I imagined she would wish for wavy dark hair or something. To my utter shock, Andrea said she wanted to alter not just one but several parts of her body. She is not alone. There are girls in her high school who have already had breast implants and nose jobs.

Somewhere God is crying. He cries for all the perfectly individual aspects of his creation that we have removed so we could conform to some manufactured ideal.

If you were to look at one of my old photo albums, you would find one picture of me hugging my baby sister so tight her eyes are bulging out and another of me on my birthday answering the door in my party dress and diaper. You'd find a Christmas photo where I am playing a toy guitar with a cowboy hat on and one of me at thirteen with a bad case of acne. These are the photos my mother loves. Her love for me does not seek a cultural picture of perfection but embraces the beauty of her own image and likeness. I'm part her and part my father. I am also made in the image of God.

It should be no surprise that God feels the same way about me. He doesn't want me to mess with a good thing. In his book

I'm a "10." I believe that even on my days of "morning face," limp and lifeless hair, and extra weight, I am only a surface away from what makes me amazing to him.

When my husband and I met, I was forty-one. He says, "I knew I had to get to know you because you walked into the room like you owned it." Maybe he's on to something in the way to look for beauty. Maybe true beauty, the beneath-the-surface kind, has more to do with the way I enter a room and the way I leave it than how I fit into what I wear. Maybe it does have something to do with my passion and sense of style and the expectancy in my step—and the magnitude of my dreams. Perhaps, after all is said and done, I am beautiful because of the reflection of God and his individual print on my insides.

That's not to say it's wrong to care about appearances. P31 was known for her style and beauty. But was this found in her designer fashions or full lips? Or was it found in other things, like health and confidence?

What if instead of resolving all the time to lose those extra fifteen pounds, P31 made a resolution to drink eight glasses of water and walk for twenty minutes or to get eight hours of sleep every day? What if her beauty secret was a decision to value her own worth by eating more fruits and vegetables and fewer carbohydrates and fat and by taking care of her skin, hair, and smile?

It should be more obvious to us that it's beautiful to be healthy. God calls our bodies his temple. That means we have to treat ourselves and our bodies respectfully: take care of what we eat and how much, be good to our muscles and give them lots of oxygen, make sure we get enough sleep and drink lots of water, challenge ourselves and keep our hearts healthy, and keep stretching our bodies in order to operate more flexibly.

We live in a time when diet centers are as numerous as gas stations and everyone wants a piece of this action in the middle of this country's obesity epidemic. When the television isn't screaming about another wonder diet drug, the Food Network is encouraging us to shout "bam!" as we dust our brownies with powdered sugar. I find it strange that a whole segment of society is pumping iron while others are happily supersizing their jumbo jacks.

How much more confusion over health and beauty do we need?

Twenty years ago I was introduced to the idea of lifting weights and working out. This month I rediscovered that I feel beautiful when I sweat. When I leave after a workout, I'm the same overweight, middle-aged woman I was when I went in, but I feel lighter, more relaxed.

When I'm lifting weights and pounding the elliptical machine at my club, I feel like I'm consciously putting myself first. I'll drink more water, I'll eat more fruits and vegetables, and I'm making a resolution to be in bed at 10:00 P.M. I'll tell myself daily that this is not exercise, not dieting, not a sign of conformity—this is a beauty treatment, because sweating is beautiful.

About ten years ago I met a makeup artist who thought wrinkles were beautiful and refused to plaster them in. She thought makeup was good only if it accented an individual's beauty, and she showed me that real beauty went deep beneath the skin.

Once on an assignment for a magazine makeover article, I met another makeup artist, a tall, gorgeous woman who put me on a hydraulic bed and introduced herself as Kim as she removed my makeup and cleansed my face. There was soft music playing and a small candle lit by the bed. The room was full of beautiful artwork and cool colors. Kim moved me to a chair in front of a mirror and began studying my face. She asked about my life, who I am really, and where I wanted to go with a makeover. She shadowed and highlighted my face, applied subtle colors I never would have thought of, and found the perfect shade of lipstick for me. She said I had gorgeous eyes and showed me that one of her eyes is significantly higher on her face.

I told her that made her a Picasso.

We laughed, and when I looked in the mirror after she was finished, I gasped. I couldn't remember looking this good, not on my best summer day, not when I was falling in love, not even in candlelight at twenty-five. I had been uncovered, revealed through the use of color, light, and shadow. My smile slid across my face into the mirror, Picasso woman was dancing around the room and saying, "You're going to knock 'em dead, girl," and I was thinking, "Yeah, I am!" because she hadn't covered me in makeup. She'd revealed me with color placed strategically in all the right places.

Beauty is a reflection of the heart. I came across a story on the Internet titled "A Gift of Love" about a woman who gave birth to a son with no ears. The baby's hearing was perfect; only his appearance had been affected. One day he rushed home from school and flung himself into his mother's arms. As he cried, he blurted out, "A boy, a big boy, called me a freak."

The mother's heart broke for her son who would obviously be faced with a life of hardship and torment.

Her boy grew handsome, but although the other students liked him, he lacked confidence of his own value. His mother tried to encourage him to get out and meet people. "Show them how wonderful you are," she would say.

The boy only grew more depressed and dejected. Finally his father went to the family physician. "Can anything be done?" he asked.

"I believe I could graft on a pair of outer ears if they could be found," the doctor said. So a search began for a person who would make such a sacrifice for this young man.

Two years went by. Then one day the father told the son, "You are going to the hospital, son. Mother and I have someone who will donate the ears you need."

"Who?" the boy asked.

"It's a secret," the father said.

The operation was a success, and a new person emerged. His talents blossomed into genius, and school and college became a series of triumphs. Later he married and entered the diplomatic service.

"I must know!" he urged his father. "Who gave so much for me? I could never do enough for him." His father reminded him of his agreement—that it would remain a secret.

The years went by and the secret was kept, but a dark day did come. The boy was a man now, and he stood with his father over his mother's casket. Slowly, tenderly, his father drew back her red hair, revealing to the son the secret donor who had been kept from him so long.

"Real beauty," the father said to the son, "is not in our outward appearance, but in our hearts."

True beauty is the knowledge of what you have to give away. When Christ walked on this earth, we're told, "he had no beauty or majesty to attract us to him, nothing in his appearance that we should desire him" (Isa. 53:2). Yet Christ was uncommonly beautiful. People were drawn to him, and he changed them by uncovering the beauty in all he came in contact with. Real beauty is expensive and rare and in the fabric of our character.

It is this uncommon and real beauty that makes us responsible for our motives and our mission. It makes us honest. It tells us to move across the dance floor no matter what our proportions. It tells us that God did not create us to define ourselves by each other. He made us funny, quirky, each with a different something. He reminds us that it is often in our imperfections that he reveals our true beauty. It is often the quirky gifts of God that set our mark on the world. I haven't always felt beautiful, but in the eyes of God are snapshots of all my moments, from every angle. When he tells me *Kathy, I made you beautiful,* I understand he is not talking about a beauty that will leave me but one that is eternal and life-giving. He is talking about his exquisite strokes on my canvas that will remain forever.

Despite all the things we know about her desires, her faith, and her gifts, we have no physical descriptions of P31. Yet we assume that she was stately and handsome and that she carried herself with dignity because of the great respect afforded her in these Scriptures. It is the beauty we have seen before: the beauty in a snapshot of Mother Teresa's hands, in Billy Graham's integrity, in Dr. Martin Luther King Jr.'s vision, in the sound of Aretha Franklin singing "Spirit in the Dark." It was God's unique signature that made P31 sparkle and shimmer. Her great beauty lay in her character, kindness, and generosity of heart.

She may have been like the little red-headed girl who is teased relentlessly and made to cry because she does not fit the ideal for beauty. She is told that she is unattractive and called names like Freckle Face and Four Eyes. Her tormentors do not see that just beneath the surface, beauty of another kind is waiting to shine through. But God has all her snapshots, from every angle, and he calls her a perfect "10." Beauty, he says, is more then skin deep. It is a slow fire that burns beneath the surface. We won't find it in any human ideal but in his fearful and wonderful exception to the rule.

7

ISLANDS

Lessons in Sanctuary

She extends her hands . . . and opens her arms

It is in the shelter of each other that the people live.

IRISH PROVERB

I dreamt that I was laying in the hand of God. His face was bent over me. He smiled the way fathers do when they know they can fix what's broken. His eyes never left me as I felt the jagged rocks of pain explode upon me—stones hitting, then the stones turning to dust. The skin of God surrounded me with such inexplicable tenderness that I lay wide open to the possibility that the body of all my knowledge was no longer important—only this thing, this love that rushed toward me like a comet racing to the mark.

MY JOURNAL, 1997

THE DAY BEFORE our kids came to live with us, I got a call from a friend who reminded me that I needed to create an island for them. She was talking about our home and the need to create an atmosphere of love, comfort, and acceptance. An island is where its residents are safe, she said. It is a sanctuary where we're affirmed and free from judgment, a place crucial for healthy growth and emotional balance.

I drew from the memories of sanctuaries past and present to begin to build the Vick Island. My own family's home had a room that felt like a hug. It had an old green couch and pillows that had seen too many years of *Andy Griffith,* family meetings, and card games that lasted long past bedtime. Our laughter had settled into the cracks of the plastered ceiling, and the furniture held the impressions of our bodies like sculpture. This room was filled with the essence of family, the events we celebrated. It was the place we would fall asleep on Sunday afternoon and run to on Saturday nights after our dates. It was the least likely room in our house to win any awards for beauty, but it had a kind of intangible luster because it was a room we built together, with every disagreement and every embrace carving out its dimensions and layered upon its foundation.

As I talk with my friends about the rooms that held our families, our voices change; they are filled with the memories

80

of the places that shaped us. The gathering places of our youth were shelters that shut out the world for brief moments that allowed us to refuel and reconnect with our families, reminding us that we were a part of something greater—and we are not alone.

"I remember gathering in a kitchen full of wonderful smells at the end of the day," my friend Karen recalls. "We would debate politics there or just talk about how the day had gone. No one was too busy, and we laughed sometimes until our sides hurt."

Another friend tells me the playroom in her family home was "an all around get-into-trouble kind of room." She explains: "It stretched the length of the house and featured a red velvet couch, linoleum floors, a fireplace, and a chest freezer. The pillows from the couch were frequently used as springboards to jettison off the top of the freezer and onto the couch. In every other room of the house we had to be 'careful' (Mom's warning). Only the playroom was the exception. In the playroom we gathered to roast marshmallows and wieners in the big stone fireplace and to slide across the linoleum after a fresh application of dance wax. All seven of us watched our parents dance from behind the crack of the door, and we daily bounced on the red couch until the springs gave way."

As specialists search for ways to bring the family back into healthy balance, they acknowledge that these rooms that held us as children are a key to binding our families together today. In her book *The Shelter of Each Other*, psychologist Mary Pipher talks about the importance of creating a place of shelter in efforts to rebuild our families. She points out that we create shelter for our families by having certain rooms in our homes where we celebrate, unwind, and practice tradition and ritual; by having places we go to, like the park or beach; and by having things we do, interests that we share.

Every year we celebrate our family birthday—June 9, 1998, the day the kids moved into their bedrooms and we set out to become The Vicks. This year we all piled in the car and went out to our favorite Chinese restaurant to celebrate our fifth year together. We ordered egg foo young, dipped into our wonton soup, and then shared our favorite memories of the past year. I pushed for the sharing, knowing that sometimes kids need to be prodded to remember how rich they are with family memories.

This birthday is a testimony that it takes many small, seemingly unimportant happenings to build an island. It takes time and diligence and the knowledge that the important elements of family happen not in the seemingly important events but when no one is looking.

I have learned that creating an island does not require spending lots of money. It requires instead some deliberate, insightful thinking: What are our emotional needs, the needs of our family? Think back over the course of your life—where have you felt the safest and most creative? Most of us will recall some small, protected space: a beach house, a Montana cabin, maybe a log by a lake or huddled around a campfire telling ghost stories. My husband remembers his grandmother's house, a place filled with good smells and big overstuffed chairs.

Summers in South Dakota on my grandparents' farm were often punctuated by a trip to a small creek a half mile from the house. Large trees grew thick by its banks with their branches arched over the creek, keeping it cool in the heat. Mosquitoes swarmed and the water was filled with leeches. It was a cattle crossing, and the path had been packed down, the rocky dirt worn smooth. My sister, Cindee, and I dredged for minnows in quart canning jars and brought them home as trophies.

On the banks of the stream was a single grave for the cherished family dog, Mickey. My Uncle Duane showed me the marker where Mickey was buried, a single wooden cross stuck in the ground with small stones surrounding it. I remember the reverence in his voice for this friend he had come to love and trust, and I returned there often and contemplated the idea of Mickey being down there in the ground and the remembrance of his trust and friendship. To me the creek was hallowed ground, this stream of my childhood. I can still remember the feeling I had standing with my toes buried in its muddy banks, the safety of its cool arms shielding me from the farm chores and shading me from the scorching sun.

Mothers are our first remembrance of this kind of sanctuary.

A mother is a soft place to land, and in many ways she becomes an island. I am the place my children go when someone has hurt them and when they are sick, disappointed, or discouraged.

Last night my son called me. He was in the middle of a break while playing bass for a gig with one of his bands. He was having a tough night playing, and the band had just told him they weren't going to use him for the following night.

"Do you want to come home?" I asked him, forgetting that sometimes at nineteen what you need is just the voice of home.

"No, I just wanted to talk," he said softly.

So I listened while he dumped his disappointment. I'd heard it before—my own words when I was nineteen and the world had not been fair.

"Keep your chin up," my dad would say, and so as my conversation with Patrick came to an end, I found myself offering the same sentiment, knowing that when you are young and you have just been devalued, that is exactly what you need to hear.

Recently I asked my kids what has made the difference in living here.

"I feel like I can be myself, no matter how crazy that is," Andrea replied.

"I think it's the fact that I know you believe in me," said Patrick, who is about to go off to college.

In our house there are many islands. Some were made with purpose, and some spilled over like tiny seeds and took root. Sanctuaries like a small attic or even a window seat acknowledge my own need for solitude. Two years ago I painted my bedroom walls to look like chamois. I decorated in colors of oak, gold, and plum. When I walk into that room, it cocoons me; when I shut the door, the kids know that unless they are on fire, I am in a time out. They take messages, field callers, and keep their questions until I emerge. They protect my need for sanctuary as I in turn make islands for them.

Two years ago our family made an island together on the streets of Portland. We adopted the Blanket Coverage Ministry outreach as our family mission. Every fourth Thursday and Friday of the month we shop for, cook, and serve a meal to approximately 130 people. We decided from the beginning that instead of the usual soup and bread, we would serve what we make at home for our own family and friends. We started bringing home-cooked Sunday suppers, complete with dessert and milk. I think at first people didn't know what to think, but they enthusiastically thanked us for the wonderful meal, most coming through the line three and four times.

They were incredulous. "You made all this for us?"

One night I had baked over three hundred cookies, and when I started unpacking them, one woman in line cried out, "Look, they made us cookies—they must really love us!"

After another dinner a woman came up to me and tearfully said, "I would like to thank whoever made that peach cobbler—it tasted just like my mother's." Then she added simply, "It's been a hard week."

I got it. I knew what she was telling me. A meal can redeem the day or even the week. A taste of something in our past that made us feel safe—it is an island.

I watch my kids wash pans and count napkins, serve milk and help carry. It is more than a meal, they know firsthand. Family dinner is a ritual at our house—a request from Andrea when she came to live with us. "I want the whole family to sit down and have a meal—together," she said.

So that is what we do, regardless of schedules or projects. There is always dinner, a table, and us. This is where the family stories are spun and good food makes us warm and fills our bodies. It is where we laugh unguarded. There is no substitute and nothing I can do that is more important.

Sometimes our islands are those we love and risk with. With a leaky ballpoint pen on lined paper, my grandfather wrote me more than one hundred letters. Each began with "Dearest Kathleen" and ended with "I'm so proud of you, your loving Grandpa Boice." Sometimes the pages were out of order or had a coffee stain in the margin, but it was clear that each one was written with great purpose and love. From his big front window he described the gentle curve of land marked by an S-shaped road leading down to the mailbox on Route 7. Sometimes, pressing the pen deep, he related his loneliness, his fear of being forgotten, and his love for Jesus.

My grandfather died in a hospital bed. He never woke up from the stroke-induced coma brought on by a car accident. All four of his sons were there at his bedside. I called the hospital room and asked my father to put the phone up to my grandpa's ear.

"I don't think he can hear you," my father had said.

"I'll take that chance," was my reply. In the minutes that followed, I had to tell my grandfather good-bye. I needed to let him off the hook. We had a deal, a secret pact. I was going to marry a wonderful guy someday, and Grandpa was going to live long enough to help give me away. That was the deal. He promised me.

Some promises aren't meant to be.

I told my grandpa I loved him, that I would miss him, and that he would never be forgotten. I gently begged him to go home, to sail into the soft folds of safe harbor. All he had loved would be waiting to welcome him. I reminded him that they had been waiting a long time. I felt he could hear me, and I had the feeling he had been waiting for my call as he slipped away soon after.

A short time after his death, I had a dream that he came from heaven through the front porch screen door of the farmhouse. That door opened with a distinct squeak of age and then slammed back in place. He was young, like the grandpa of my youth, wearing a white shirt with his sleeves rolled up, dirt clinging to his fingertips and eyes lit up with excitement. He held up his hands like a surgeon.

"Kathy," he said, "it's great up here."

So I think of Grandpa up there working God's fields when my own islands seem wanting. I remember his smile and know the sanctuaries of this earth are only a shadow of what is yet to come.

The woman of Proverbs 31 was a shelter to her family, her friends, and her community. She gave those around her the hope to stand, run, succeed—the will to survive the cold. Her shelter was in the palm of God's hand, cupped in the presence of her family. She realized that islands happen with time and without fanfare.

Our purpose is to be an island for all those who are lost and to look for islands when we feel our reserves are dwindling. P31 knew that she had a God who had made her for this great task. She was his hands and feet; she could convey his heart and with it she could convince those around her that they could be islands too—a room, a garden, an altar for God. In this place only the language of truth and love is spoken. Its roots are sacred and ancient and run deep, "for Christ did not enter a man-made sanctuary that was only a copy of the true one; he entered heaven itself" (Heb. 9:24).

We were created to hunger for this intimacy and, as long as we are alive, to create islands in our living. It is there among the everyday activities of life that our weaknesses are swept away. It is a shadow of hope that one day we will be wrapped in the soft folds of God's waiting arms.

In my best moments, I remember this counsel from P31. "Sister," I hear her say, "in the islands God creates, all your striving will be no more—only his love, his safe and warm comfort stretched out—all this rushes toward you like a comet racing to the mark."

8

STORMS

Lessons in Forgiveness and Endurance

She is clothed with . . . dignity

Life is an adventure in forgiveness.

NORMAN COUSINS,
SATURDAY REVIEW

THE WORST GALES in my life have been tempests of the heart. They have swept through my life like hurricanes, throwing my existence around like a rag doll and temporarily altering my vistas. They have taught me that without perseverance, without sheer refusal to be trapped in my own hatred, I would have to fight with every weapon I could learn to use or I would become just another casualty of life.

Hatred was the ultimate trap; the wound was a black chasm of frustration turned to hurt, turned to bitterness, turned to rage, and my pain was endless. During the day I loathed my oppressor, and at night I dreamed of perpetrating cruel acts of revenge. I was consumed by my own vileness and self-loathing.

I prayed to God for relief, but he grew silent.

I begged for escape, and he whispered—not quite loud enough, I thought.

Then in desperation, on my knees, I cried out to him for release.

He told me to build an altar in my heart and to lay there all my rights, to put all my hopes for vindication in his hands. Give it up, he said. You cannot bear it.

So it is with forgiveness every day. Finally, almost ten years ago, I recognized this and wrote as a prayer in my journal, "I rebuild this place and hand it to you, God. I give you all the things that would trap and enslave me so that I can live the way you called me—free."

Forgiveness is an act of radical endurance. It tests our relationship with an unseen God in a very tangible way. It is an act of giving over your rights to something bigger, much bigger. For most of us this doesn't come easy. After all, forgiveness begins with the act of acknowledging that we are overwhelmed. Someone has hurt us and we cannot fathom why. *How could they do this to me? Don't they realize how valuable I am?* We have the sense that if they just knew what they had done, they would be sorry and it could somehow be undone.

Then, without warning, the hurt turns to anger. We believe that the person who has hurt us deserves to be hated, and we deserve to be vindicated. We sense that if we let go, the person who has wounded us is somehow taken off the hook. So the anger turns to hatred, and the trap is snapped on us. We clutch our hatred tightly, as though it is something to sustain us. We feed on it, even though it turns our stomach sour; in our darkness, our soul hungers for it until we are paralyzed by bitterness.

I write this from experience. I have felt these bitter stabbings. I have been this hurt, angry woman. And I know others.

Did P31 ever taste bitterness? Did she forgive those who attacked, judged, and compared her?

Several years ago I went with *Virtue* magazine to the Oregon State Penitentiary women's prison in Salem to give a workshop on forgiveness. I sat in a small recreation room with about twenty women. I remember thinking first that they looked so young. I saw that a couple young girls were pregnant. Several had tattoos and showed signs of past heroin addictions. One young woman had pulled out all the hair on the side of her head.

Their faces made me love them. These were women in pain, wounded and desperate, and I recognized the look in their eyes.

I told them my own story, a story that so easily could have ended like theirs. My hatred was so strong—I felt at times that I was inches away from acting out my revenge. I shared with them how the hatred wearied me until I could no longer deal with it and felt forced to give it to God. As I spoke, I could see recognition grow in their eyes.

When I finished, the women filed out the door, quieter, more subdued. One woman stayed behind, the woman who had torn out her own hair. She asked me in a matter-of-fact voice, "Did you know that at least eleven of the women in the group have committed murder?" Then she began to cry as she told me her own story—a story of fear that revenge would be taken on her by those she had wounded. I couldn't help but think that there are many views of forgiveness, and that at one time or another we see them all. Sometimes we are the victims, some of us unknowingly will be the victimizers, and sometimes we become the defenders of those who have been unjustly dealt pain.

My kids miss their biological mother. They have not seen her for four years. Birthdays come and there is a silent hope they will get a call from her.

Sometimes they ask me, "I know it's stupid, but do you think Mom will call?"

I stroke their faces or a shoulder or a back. "It's not stupid to hope that she is thinking of you," I say.

Then, when the call doesn't come, their faces show the strain of being overwhelmed, of not being able to comprehend how their mother could forget them. They are desperate. Yet I know there is more than one side to this story. Their mother must be desperate too . . . but it is hard to forgive.

Three years ago my sister and I hurt each other. It was our first Christmas together after my marriage. We arrived while she was still cleaning the house. She had been consumed with writing and directing a play that would be performed at the Center for the Arts in Escondido on Christmas Eve. The house showed evidence of many unfinished projects, and I stepped into it feeling angry. Someone had been on the phone while I was trying to call to get the security gate opened. I was stressed. She was stressed. It was a bad beginning to an even worse week.

At the end of the holiday we both were mad and each felt righteously justified, so for two years we rarely spoke. The wound just went deeper, and although many times I tried to figure out what might change the situation, I was overwhelmed. It was outside of my own ability to fix what was wrong. All I could do was pray. It wasn't as simple as calling my sister and asking forgiveness; it was timing and conditions. I recognized that I had to wait. Finally a day came when my eyes were opened to my own sin—my own part in this long-standing competition and feud that hadn't just started two years before but had essentially been with us all our lives.

A week before Thanksgiving, I sat down and wrote her a letter, fully intending to send it to her. It was a letter I would never send. It stayed on my dresser while I continued to pray to God, because I reasoned I had always been the peacemaker.

I pleaded with God, "I'd like her to make the first move."

I didn't hold out a lot of hope for that. In fact, I thought I very well might be in rebellion by waiting, because after all, God had told me to write the letter.

It sat on my dresser, and every day I would think about it and feel like maybe I would send it, but I never did. Ten days later I got a call from my sister. She didn't say hello or how have you been; there was no small talk. She softly uttered these words: "Kathy, I cannot live without you—I don't want to live without you. Would you please forgive me?"

There are no words that can compare. None. I will never forget the tears that came until both of us were sobbing into the phone. As long as I live I will cherish that phone call. There is nothing sweeter to our ears than the word *forgiveness*—and no bigger test of our faith.

Hurt, anger, disillusionment—none of us is exempt from the wounds of a friend, a relative, a husband, or a parent. We will see these things, feel them, and taste their bitterness from all vantage points, and we will call out to God for relief.

He shows us that here are two distinctly separate paths; one leads to life and the other to death. To travel down the path of life, we must forgive. On this road there are words like *happiness, success, freedom,* and *fulfillment.* On the path to death are words like *hatred, depression, addiction, failure,* and *disappoint-*

ment. God asks us to forgive so that we may be forgiven and to make forgiveness our lifestyle. We forgive not because everyone deserves to be let off the hook, but because God says we deserve to be people who live in forgiveness. A clause in our contract with God reads, "but if you do not forgive, neither will your Father who is in heaven forgive your sins" (Mark 11:26).

I strive daily to fulfill my contract with God, but honestly, on my own I can't forgive. I can't forgive Pat's ex-wife for hurting my kids so deeply with her choices and in the process turning my life upside down. I can't forgive words spoken that cut me down or leave me feeling judged. I can't forgive my neighbor who allows his dog to use my front lawn as a bathroom every morning. I can't forgive . . . I can't without the assistance and intervention of the Holy Spirit, who opens me up to the possibility that until I let go, God cannot be my vindicator.

When I give God my rights for revenge, it puts him on the job. You may never know just how he vindicated you because his take on revenge is, well, godly. "Do not take revenge, my friends, but leave room for God's wrath, for it is written: 'It is mine to avenge; I will repay,' says the Lord" (Rom. 12:19).

What that means is "Don't look back." When you are tempted to imagine what God should or will do to vindicate you, resist the temptation. Your rights were surrendered when you gave him the whole deal; you must do this every new day. You must repeat, "God, this is too ugly and too big to resolve on my own. Please clean it up for me."

On my visit to the women's prison, I got up to sing. My knees were knocking as I approached the front, but once the first word passed over my lips, I forgot my nervousness and let the song flow from my heart. There are songs in this world that you simply can't sing unless you have come through hard places. This was such a song and such a time.

The women I was singing to began to slowly pass a roll of toilet paper up and down the aisles. They each took a piece, like communion, and dabbed their eyes. I finished to only the sound of women sobbing. Some women didn't even try to muffle their cries.

Whether we are the ones that mess up or the ones who were messed over, "I Surrender All" is our song. The words reflect the end result of a lifestyle of forgiveness: "All to Jesus, I surrender; Lord, I give myself to Thee. Fill me with Thy love and power; let Thy blessing fall on me."

When all is said and done, that is what we really need on the other side of our storms. We need God's blessing; we need to feel the redemptive power of the blessing fall on us from our head to our toes, assuring us that no matter what may come to test us, he has the power to redeem it, to bless us, and that is why it really doesn't matter how God chooses to vindicate us—what matters is what happens to our hearts in the process.

P31 was no different, and for her to be clothed with strength and dignity meant she may have had more than her share of pain. True strength, we are taught, comes from acknowledging our weakness and leaning on God, and true dignity comes from the humility of acknowledging our own sin. She wore her strength and dignity because it kept her true to her calling to stay free. She knew nothing was a greater threat to her freedom than the trap of unforgiveness.

God waits for us to be desperate because only a desperate heart will do whatever it takes. God uses that brokenness to play out his great story of redemption and to restore our hearts. Some of us will learn the first time around, but for those like me it will mean circling the drain several times to realize that forgiveness is the only way to get free—to stay buoyant. What I have learned is that God wants our desperate hearts, that he promises that he is "close to the brokenhearted; he rescues those who are crushed in spirit" (Ps. 34:18 NLT). It is our desperation that makes us hand the keys over to him. We do not have to believe the one we are forgiving deserves forgiveness, only that we are desperate to be someone who forgives. It is the ticket price of entering into the circle of grace and regaining our equilibrium of heart.

Forgiveness is an act of radical faith. It tests the reality of our relationship with God. For most of us it doesn't come easy; we have hurts that are deep and ragged. Deciding to forgive is one step toward a life of buoyancy; it is the second chance to go to the dance, to be happy—not just Sunday-at-church happy but, as my daughter would say, "the-whole-camole" happy.

The worst storms in my life have been the storms of my heart, and God has shown me that nothing can blow me down because I live with a God who redeems and vindicates. I have seen it with my own eyes and through the eyes of women who thought they could never be forgiven. There is blessing for a life surrendered to God; it falls like gentle rain and promises to make everything clean and new. It is the sound of freedom.

9

WILD WIND

Lessons in Our Inheritance

She is like the merchant ships

One can never consent to creep when one feels an impulse to soar.

HELEN KELLER

THE SEA IS a wild arena, and the winds do not ask how hard they can blow—their strength is in the untamed spirit given to them when God collected the waters and gave them his breath. Through the winds he demonstrates not only his own wild nature, but the wild strength he has placed in all his creation.

Yesterday I watched a television interview with an Arab king. Dressed in a *kaffiyeh* (headdress traditionally worn by Arabs), he strikes me as a man who holds the world in his pocket. There is a smirk on his face, and his dark eyes fill with light. His face creases at places that reveal his age. He is discussing the changing opportunities for Saudi women; his mind is on the future of his own daughters. "I think women will take what is theirs regardless of what we do," he says. Then he smiles again and says, "Who could deny them what is theirs?"

In other words: You watch, my daughters will be as relentless as the wild wind.

I think God speaks with the same confidence in the inherent strength and tenacity of his daughters. Who will block their destinies? My daughters don't need permission, and they don't offend; they don't fight gender battles, and they don't ask for opinions or look for affirmation. They are powered by something so clearly theirs that the challengers step out of the way, the walls crumble, and the enemy is blinded. Why would my daughters fight for an inheritance that is already theirs? If I gave one a gift for speaking, who can stand in her way? If I gave another a gift of leadership, who could possibly keep her from leading?

Most of the barriers and obstacles to discovering my own strength have not been other people. I'm not saying that other people didn't play minor roles in this drama, but the real enemy was and is always going to be me. The truth is, I have not always been strong. I have been a bully and I have been the one bullied, but the true strength of a woman and the wild, tenacious nature of God eluded me.

I grew up timid and shy. My family moved every couple of years. It was like someone handing me a bus ticket and a new identity and then telling me to make a new life. There were always new styles, new schools, new friends and teachers, new churches and neighbors. It was exhausting. The first few days were the worst. The experience was the classic humiliation of the new girl. "Have you seen the new girl? Have you seen the chubby, four-eyed new girl?" In retrospect, I should have sold tickets.

Then there were the notes passed to me with disparaging comments like "dog face" and the physical torment, the beatings after school on the way home, being pushed into bushes and down hills, being laughed at and shunned by the people who mattered. I learned to be a chameleon, to be invisible, to move through a crowd undetected. I used my best stealth skills to remain benign in every way. My opinions went unnoticed, my style was brown everything. And if I had stayed that way, I would have been a woman who didn't know her own strength. I would have been that woman if it hadn't been for Mom.

My mother stands five feet, two inches in her bare feet. From my childhood I remember her as a quiet, shy woman with mousy brown hair and big cornflower blue eyes. She smiled a lot. She let Dad have the spotlight as he told his jokes and stories, most of them ending with laughter and adoration.

In the sixties and seventies my mother went through some changes. First, she started attending college, found a group of women who were mutually supportive, and came to the startling realization that she was brilliant. Her quiet days came to an abrupt halt. It was sometime in these days of reckoning that my mother began to tell me, "Kathy, you can achieve whatever you set your heart and mind on."

It was like fuel, a slow, consistent blessing that gathered in my gut, down at the base of my knowledge of who I was.

In the summer of 1962, I went to stay on my grandparents' farm. My Grandma Boice filled our days with chores and crafts, everything from rolling large squares of beeswax into candles to making Popsicle stick trivets. She herded cattle in a baby blue '61 Chevy Impala. She drove at breakneck speeds over the jagged South Dakota hills, looking every bit a history book pioneer woman. She had rough hands and thick eyebrows that had never seen tweezers. She was tough in the best sense, not in a mean or ugly way. Grandma never let anything hold her back. Even the rocks gave way to her as she maneuvered the Chevy through the fields. She was fierce, and as I sat next to her on the slick vinyl seats, clutching the door for my life, my admiration and loyalty were sealed forever.

One day in July, Grandma bought me a paint-by-number kit. It featured a ballerina standing *en pointe* in pastels of pinks and blues. I was immediately captivated, and so I began to paint each numbered area with the appropriate color. I followed the plan meticulously. When it was finished, I began to paint my own ballerinas, one after another, until little canvases littered the house.

My next year at school was tough. I was in a new school again, and the punishing abuse for being the new girl had escalated to my being relegated to the classroom during recess for my own safety.

One day my mother got a call from my teacher. "I was wondering, does Kathy have any talents or special gifts that we could highlight in class so the kids will get to see her in a different light?"

My mother told her of my newfound love of painting ballerinas, so it was decided that I would paint during recess. One day after all my classmates had come back in from recess, I noticed that my teacher had put my ballerina paintings up all around the room. "Class," she said, "we have a real artist among us."

As the students scanned the room, they were stunned. The questions flew. "How did you do it?" "Where did you learn?" I was a real artist, and for the first time I was beginning to see what made me both beautiful and strong.

The tracks left by that old Chevy and Grandma disappeared long ago, but here in me are the indelible treads of strength that she passed to me without blinking. I will forever be in her debt for finding the real me—the strong and passionate me—in a paint-by-number kit on a summer afternoon. It raised my expectations of myself, and by the time I was in high school, I was losing my chameleon skin and beginning to feel my own strength and power.

I remember a defining moment: I walked through some double doors in my high school only to discover I was flanked by two rows of boys. The boys were shouting out scores, holding up numbered cards judging all the girls walking through their gauntlet. I was immediately paralyzed at facing what I felt was yet another inevitable humiliation.

At the end of the hall I saw Mr. McAllister, my creative writing teacher. He was the kind of teacher all the girls secretly had crushes on, giggling into their clammy hands every time he walked by.

Seeing my plight, he sprinted to my side and began to waltz with me down the hallway. He sang, "Strangers in the night, exchanging glances," at the top of his lungs as he danced me in circles, taking his time, singing with so much verve and passion that I began to giggle and throw back my head. I glanced at my would-be judges, who stood gaping in silence, their mouths loose and wordless, their rating cards hanging by their sides.

This is how it feels, I thought, *to not be invisible.*

I made a secret choice to never be invisible again.

I believe that God is standing at the end of all our hallways. He alone knows our true strength. He sees us standing there alone, about to be judged, trampled, and humiliated. He begins to dance with us, slowly and purposefully, so that everyone can see the folly of their unbelief in us. He uses the element of surprise to throw the enemy off balance and to uncover us, his secret weapon. He is astute in the ways of guerilla warfare, studying an obstacle and finding the best way around it. He uses his secret weapon—us—to put us in places of power and influence. He sways the minds of kings (see the story of Esther, Esther 5–7). He provides us with an inheritance (see the story of Ruth, Ruth 2–3). He uses our extravagant acts of compassion to teach the world about love (see the story of the woman who anointed Jesus, Matthew 26:6–13). And he made us the first to see God's redemption (see the story of Elizabeth meeting Mary, Luke 2:39–45).

Because God unmasks those who stand in my way, I can be obedient to how he tells me to travel. Do not look to your own strength, but look to the strength that I give you, he says. Do not bully your way into job opportunities or relationships, but be ready, study which way the wind is blowing, meditate on my ways, wait for my anointing, and I will make you as resilient as the mighty reed that bends but never breaks. Let me move you into places of influence and power; I will use you to change the surface of things. He says, "Be careful to obey every command I am giving you today, so you may have strength to go in and occupy the land you are about to enter" (Deut. 11:8 NLT)—because before you can sit in these places I've prepared for you, you are going to have to know what you're made of.

At fifteen, my daughter exudes the tenacity of an animal with prey. The girl knows how to fight, knows how to defend herself. What she struggles with is what is at her core.

I tell her, "Andrea, there is nothing you can't do if you put your mind and heart to it."

My mother's litany has now become mine. In time, I pray, it will be like fuel, and as the years dance by like my paint-by-number ballerinas, Andrea will come to know what lies beneath her skin, what she can draw from, and what makes her strong.

P31 was strong in her core; she moved freely in a society that was especially rigid. In the words of her story, P31 does not seem to need permission to sell her field and plant a vineyard. She did not gather all those in leadership at the temple to decide if she could have a ministry to the poor and needy. It says she "feared the Lord," which infers it was this part of her character that set her in high places among the influencers and the people who made things happen in her community. She faced life with the question of "What if?" instead of "Do you think I could?"

P31 shows us that our purpose is to be heroines, tenacious and strong. It is our inheritance to ride this wild wind, to discover what strength God breathed on us. We do not need permission; we do not need to seek affirmation. We were made in secret, part of God's arsenal. Placed in our grasp is the strength to move mountains or to circumvent them, to break the rules without offending. God himself dresses us for our assignments.

My family album holds a picture of me in a T-shirt that says POWER TO WOMEN on it. I am eighteen years old, and it is 1974. In the picture I am hamming it up, making a power sign with my fist. It is clear in the picture that I didn't have a clue what power really meant.

Today I see that true strength is what God accomplishes through me and in me. It is the knowledge that I am solid, impregnable, God's daughter looking to him for my strategy. My strength is not just a matter of accomplishing my own goals but of being part of a larger purpose. It is being a mom or a mentor. It is being part of the overall strength of all women by holding up what is true and godly, by reaching with compassion and wisdom into my community. My own achievements will be forgotten, but the residuals of my strength will continue through all women. I see that there will be those who would judge me, contain me, or fear me, but I also know that they will become slack-mouthed and wordless at the motion of God's mighty hand. I have found great comfort in God's big picture, because in it women are strong.

Two years ago I gave a book to my mother for Christmas and vowed (half seriously) that I was going to write a book and dedicate it to her, although I didn't know that the subject matter would be motherhood. My vow didn't surprise her. I don't think she ever doubted anything I've ever done. She taught me to ask "what if?" and I stopped getting permission a long time ago.

I try to pass this on to my daughter and to all the daughters of a living God who calls us by a new name and gives us his inheritance. In me is his own wild nature and the wild strength he has placed in all his creation. God brought me here.

I believe that God is waiting for me at the end of the hallway like Mr. McAllister, waltzing me into opportunities of his choosing and revealing that through him I can both thunder down a mountain and bend like the reed.

10

STILLNESS

Lessons in God's Presence

She gets up while it is still dark

Blow on this place,
Where I hide in my fear,
Carry me gently,
To a stream far from here.

Where your voice is the water,
A sweet tide of peace.
It rocks me and soothes me,
Every thought I release.

Remind me again,
That you know I can fly?
That I'll see things of Heaven,
If I open my eyes?

In this stillness between us,
I find the hush of your grace.
As you give me the power
To finish this race.

KATHY VICK

I WAS STANDING in the swift waters of the St. Joe River. Just beyond me the water dumped into a deep green pool. It was trout water. With my first cast, a rainbow trout met my fly before it kissed the surface. Nine sequined, silver fins followed, jumping to the dance of my line. All nine were released by my own hand. There was no sound but the music of the river, no smell but acrid pine and rich, dark earth. Far above I heard the gentle rustling of the wind in the trees and then a hush. I was filled with a consuming joy of stillness. Beneath my feet, rocks slick with moss reminded me that this was ephemeral. I could not stay in this place, and as I balanced there, poised for the next cast, my heart broke with that knowledge.

I carry the memory of water. Perhaps it is my need, like the waters, to circulate and refresh. To have the clean, clear water flow through me, erasing my furrowed brow and buoying the smallness of my faith. My life does not easily make way for this kind of reflection; I am not still by nature. My days are full of lists and needs, and yet these days I realize that I am thirsty. My heart is parched, and I confess to you that it has been far too easy to come to this place. I long to feel the presence of God—to confide in him like an old friend who knows my shortcomings but still finds me fascinating, to be quenched by his words, to hear them in my head and feel them in my soul. My life has become a series of reactions to the administration of my family, my home, and my marriage, and I ache to return to the edge of my river.

It is hard to stop. It is more difficult to listen—and harder still to simply know that God is who he says he is. Frankly, stillness often seems like something that requires too much planning, too much energy. Some days I am afraid to sit down for fear that I may never get up again.

As I write this, it is 8:00 A.M. My daughter is an hour late for school, my husband is sick and will need a ride to the doctor, my son is cooking eggs, and I hope he will remember to turn off the burner. My retriever, Carmella, is lying at my feet so that I will remember that she needs to be fed and walked. When you are at the center of a family's world, it is often hard to find that still place. I hunger for the quiet waters, to feel my life all stretched out like the glassy tendons of the St. Joe—to watch and listen and reconnect with the simple joy of being.

My life was not always like this. I used to have time to reflect, to read, to write in my journal, to paint, and to dream—that was before I was married with children. My married friends used to salivate over the fact that I could read an entire book—in one day—and had time to celebrate myself, time to travel and to light candles at the end of each day. Today I am realizing that if I need stillness, I will need to schedule it in.

The author of the Psalms speaks to us of an old invitation to be led to a place where I shall want nothing, where I will lie down in green pastures, and where I can walk hand in hand with God beside the waters of peace. Long before the last great glacier retreated, leaving the Great Lakes and a stream called the St. Joe River, God knew of my need for waters. He has known from my beginnings that I would seek to find this place and has given me a promise that if I am still, he will unveil the waters of peace in the middle of my life. God calls me to stillness because he knows that without it I will live parched and thirsty.

Every year my husband and I schedule a trip to Glacier National Park. We bundle up in front of the East Glacier Lodge fireplace and listen to the crackling giant logs. We sit out on the veranda that travels the expanse of the lodge and gaze on the Continental Divide, admiring the pinks and lavenders of a sunset or the moon that seems so close we can touch it. We sit until the stars fill the sky and we can no longer see the great range looming before us. We dream of what God has for us as we cast our goals before him and listen to the wind in the giant trees.

One year we missed our Glacier trip. We felt it all year long. It felt like being left behind and not quite knowing how to reconnect with the travel agenda. We felt out of harmony with our life, at times with each other. We grumbled about it all year long and promised we would never miss Glacier again. So every year we go just before the lodge closes and the first snows come, and we reflect on what the year has brought and what is yet to come.

Stillness is a decision we make every day to gather our energies. We all have to find our own way to practice stillness. Some use a daily meditation or study, some go into a prayer time, others listen to tapes in their car on the way to work, and still others walk, hike, or run. Everyone has to find a way to fuel up for the day ahead because, the psalmist reminds us, "My eyes are always looking to the Lord for help, for he alone can rescue me from the traps of my enemies" (Ps. 25:15 nlt). God tells us that every day there will be traps, things that will try to take our energies and rob us of the peace that he gives us.

Last night my son accidentally threw my favorite amethyst earrings into the garbage disposal, which mangled them beyond recognition. My husband brought them to me for positive identification while I was getting ready for bed. He presented them to me all laid out like two tiny bodies. With the seriousness of a coroner, he said, "I think I have some bad news for you, Mrs. Vick. Tell me these aren't your earrings." This morning I found my daughter sitting in the dark watching music videos wearing jeans, a black beanie, and a black hooded sweatshirt with the hood up. "What's going on with the hair?" I said. I was answered with a half hour litany about how this was "her style," and would I please stop trying to insist that she be girlie and just listen, which I found humorous since I rarely talk before my first cup of coffee. This is the kind of little irritant that is thrown in my path every day. They aren't big or life-threatening events, but they are constant, like water tapping on your head until you want to run screaming through the house.

Stillness is my response to the little snares of my life. Four months ago we adopted a seven-year-old retriever named Carmella, and every day since then at 8:30 a.m. I have walked her down to the duck pond. There, while Carmella watches the ducks and geese, I unravel my heart before God. I open my hands so that the worries of the day can tumble down freely. "Help me, Lord, to love and care for my kids, and by the way, I think something died in my son's room." "Help me write honestly, support my husband, and be more grateful for the day." I shake loose my need to control, my rights, and my anxious thoughts. "God, are you still there? Could you maybe send me some kind of acknowledgment?" Like a cool hand on my forehead, God whispers, "I believe in your life. Go now, and be amazing."

When you first learn to sail, you spend a lot of time dead in the water. Sailing depends on sails, wind, and skill. Most people imagine sailing like the pictures in magazines, people smiling, wind in their hair, sails filled. What people don't realize is that you also spend an incredible amount of time just sitting there. My sister and I would pray out loud for wind on those days when the water was glassy and the heat beat down on our backs.

I've spent a lot of time praying for wind in my life. Stillness sometimes feels like you are dead in the water. Most of the time the subject matter of my prayers is the same and I cannot see the small wake behind us as God moves us forward on a thimbleful of wind. Time passes, and one day the things we are praying about click and we can see that we have arrived at a different place.

I prayed for compassion toward my son for months before I saw that I was penalizing him for being like his mother. I sat for years praying that God would help me lose weight until I saw that my extra pounds were not about food but about self-protection. God has filled my sails, restoring my strength and adjusting my heart. The wind blusters over the toxins of my sin and blows clean on my soul. I watch the tell tails of the mainsail and the flutter of the burgee, and I wait for God to blow.

There was a time in my life that I particularly felt dead in the water. I was unemployed, single, and anxious about pretty much everything in my life. I didn't know where I was going or what I wanted to do. That is, until I realized that I had enough frequent flyer miles to go to Italy. I got on a plane with my friend Laurie, and we flew to Milan with plans to be in Sorrento on Valentine's Day. Our plans to go to Sorrento were crushed because of a rail strike. Instead, on Valentine's Day I found myself in a small chapel in Siena surrounded by posted signs that said NO TOURISTS ALLOWED. But it was a church, I reasoned, and I was no tourist. I sat in the back while a parish priest performed the Valentine's Day mass in Latin. I didn't need the words; all I wanted was this place of stillness and reflection in the middle of my altered dreams. Later I wrote in my journal, "God whispers to me, 'Be still and know that I am God.'" I told him how much I loved him for giving me this trip in the midst of life, for not abandoning me during my ugliness and, I will confess, my lack of faith.

Did P31 ever feel dead in the water? Was she ready for the little snares of her life? Did she ever ask God the hard questions that had no easy answers? Was she thirsty for his words? We know that she rose early so she could rest in God on the precipice of her day. She found a still and quiet place where she could adjust and prioritize the day's requirements. I think she held onto the sails even when she couldn't feel any movement. She waited for the whisper of wind that would propel her forward. She looked toward the horizon, expectant to find waters that would fill her with peace in the middle of her day. She watched with all her senses over the affairs of her household and directed the work at hand. Although we don't know the specific things she struggled with, my guess is that they were not that different than the things that fill our days. To be a woman to be praised, she had to find her own place of stillness.

In our buoyancy act, God calls us to be still. "In repentance and rest is your salvation; in quietness and trust is your strength" (Isa. 30:15). He tells us that it is important to sit by still waters, because we do not know what the day will require of us. God assures that there are things that will ensnare us, but he has a way of escape. "We have escaped like a bird out of the fowler's snare; the snare has been broken, and we have escaped" (Ps. 124:7). Or it is as if he says, "There's a change in the wind coming, so hold tight to your sails and watch for me." He admonishes us to be willing to center each day on him.

The St. Joe River rises and falls without me these days, but I get up early and meet God by the duck pond. I like to think that P31 had a duck pond too. I imagine that she laid herself open to God so that her words could be sweet and kind in the midst of mangled amethyst earrings and fifteen-year-old girls

116

in hoodies. From all accounts P31 was on top of her game, every day. She inspires and awes me, because I know what it is to travel the very fine line between sainthood and insanity. I pray that one day my kids will know what it took and that forever I will be able to walk by the waters, sailing from here to there with the assurance of my place in God's heart.

11

LIFELINE

Lessons in Trust

Her husband has full confidence in her

Marriage is an Authentic weaving together of families, of two souls with their individual fates and destinies, of time and eternity—everyday life married to the timeless mysteries of the soul.

THOMAS MOORE, *SOUL MATES*

THE WORST SQUALL in twenty-five years blew into the Chesapeake Bay without warning. It hit us at rocket speeds and took down boats all around us like toothpicks. My father stood on the bow trying to unhook the sail, waves crashing over him so violently that at times I couldn't see him. I suddenly realized he wasn't wearing a lifeline. Sheer fear and will propelled me up onto the deck where I wrapped my arms around his legs, lying flat on the deck. I told him I wasn't letting go. He screamed at me to get below. I didn't move. The harder the storm blew, the harder it thrashed us, the more tenacious was my grip. When the storm subsided, we discovered that we were one of a handful of boats to escape being capsized.

In sailing a lifeline is made of nylon rope; in marriage it is woven with the fragile twines of trust. It is a risky venture, because as humans we occasionally blow it. As though marriage wasn't fearful enough, I used to have a recurring dream that kept me steeled for the very worst. I would dream that on my wedding day, I'd suddenly realize that my groom was an imposter. Sometimes I would dream that he would arrive for the wedding looking nothing like the man I had been engaged to. He would be dressed in a geeky tuxedo, goofy clown shoes, and horrific thick glasses held together by electrical tape. Other times I would dream that I discovered he was wanted by the FBI. It always happened the moment before I walked down the aisle. I was left standing with my father, trying to decide what to do, in a mixture of disappointment, grief, and anger. I would wake up in a sweat, feeling emotions of betrayal and broken trust.

Let's face it: It is really hard to trust in an age of fluctuating integrity where telemarketers and advertisers invade our privacy only to say "trust us." Our politicians' frailties are exposed, our courts fail to keep us safe, and our governments withhold secret information. Clergy and teachers are caught breaking intimate trust. A pedophile may likely be living in your neighborhood, your identity could be compromised by someone lurking at a computer screen hundreds of miles away, and every fifteen seconds a woman is beaten by someone she trusts. We are living in a time the headlines very well could read NOBODY REALLY TRUSTS ANYBODY ANYMORE. So how do we create trust in our lives? How do we know who to trust?

When I met my husband, I asked myself, *Can I trust him?* Is he an honest man, ethical in business and money? Will he be faithful to me? Will he tell me the truth while protecting my ego? Christ knew this very familiar human dilemma. He struggled in his trust of humans, for he knew our weaknesses and could see our true motives. "Who do you say I am?" he would ask (Matt. 15:16). Indeed it was continually surprising who they thought he was; they could not be trusted to understand him. Christ himself teaches us about how to set boundaries with those we don't trust: "But Jesus would not

121

entrust himself to them, for he knew all men. . . . When he had finished speaking, Jesus left and hid himself from them" (John 2:25; 12:36).

Recently a single friend said to me, "It must be wonderful to know you can trust your husband." I told her that I trust Pat because I've watched him return to a restaurant when he was undercharged a dollar for soup. I've seen him on countless occasions follow through on commitments to help friends because he had given "his word." I've seen his faithfulness, and long before I married him, he showed me he was worthy of my trust. He showed me by calling when he said he was going to call and being where he told me he was going to be. He showed me in riskier ways by sharing with me tough issues of finances and children that he wanted me to know about before I married him. More than all of this, I trust him because I know he sees me, not just with his eyes but with a depth and breadth that constantly astounds me. He gets it—he understands what I'm made of.

The hard truth about trust is that it has to be earned. We never really know if we truly can have confidence in someone until we see them act in trustworthy ways. I met Pat seven years ago. When he met me he had a bouquet of flowers and a smile that disarmed me. By our third kiss I freaked myself out by turning to him and saying, "Do you think you're going to marry me or something?" I remember he immediately answered, "Yes, I think I am." We just stood there looking at each other, wondering what had just happened. And then we laughed. I don't know if we were laughing because we were

caught off guard or because we both realized we had miraculously found each other. Still, the knowledge that I could trust
him would not come for quite some time.

In marriage the harder question may be, *How honest am I?*
Often the search for more honesty and trust in our lives begins
with facing ourselves and getting honest about who we are.
God tells us that honesty is a gesture of love: "An honest answer
is like a kiss on the lips" (Prov. 24:26). I figure this honesty
is important in all my relationships. If I want to build a life
that is based on trust and honesty, I must be willing to look
at the cracks of my life that aren't working, the places where
I have been trapped by my own self-deception.

"Do you think vampires are real?" I asked my kids one day
after they had been watching *Buffy the Vampire Slayer.* Andrea
immediately rolled her eyes and replied, "No." Patrick, on the
other hand, half joking, started to tell me he was becoming
light sensitive and might have to start wearing special glasses
during the day. I attempted the question again: "Do you think
there are people who are *like* vampires in our lives?" We talked
about people they had encountered in school and in their past
who had lied to them, exhausted them, and made them feel
bad. The conclusion was that there are indeed "real" vampires
in our lives, and they have been there since the beginning of
time. They are far more dangerous than the vampires on TV
because they trap us in distrust and impede us from being
honest about our own lives.

There have been vampires in my life. When I hit my thirties, I came to the startling realization of what a boundary was

123

and set out to create some in my life. So I severed a lot of ties with friends who left me exhausted or consistently made me feel bad—people I didn't really trust. I gave up "cool" friends who were users and "victim" friends who were sucking the life out of me. Then I sat down and realized I was incredibly lonely. You don't just make a change like that overnight. In the weeding-out process, you begin asking yourself the harder question, and that is, Why am I attracting these people in the first place? I began to see that I got a lot of power by telling people how to fix their lives, and that it conveniently took all the pressure off the problems in my own life. I saw that in order to be liked by the "cool" people, I was willing to be used, and that it took the pressure off figuring out what I really wanted.

Honesty and trust begin with how we see ourselves and how we conduct ourselves when no one is looking. It takes extreme trust in God and great inner work to deal with the lies we have fed ourselves about how good we are. Isaiah puts it this way: "You have trusted in your wickedness and have said, 'No one sees me.' Your wisdom and knowledge mislead you when you say to yourself, 'I am, and there is none besides me'" (Isa. 47:10). In other words, my only hope to have an honest life is to give myself over to God. The other option is to be fooled by a series of illusions.

Every year there is a sand castle contest in Cannon Beach, Oregon. On a day in early June, teams arrive in trucks with various forms of equipment, each of them intent on building the very best sculpture on the beach. In just a few hours, sand

124

giants will make their debut. Everything from mermaids and aliens to condos and castles will rise from the sand. As the sun sets, the beach empties, and by morning the sand castles will be nothing but giant lumps. Some relationships in my life have been like sand castles. They were built on less than real foundations. Where there isn't trust, there is dishonesty. It may be about small things, unimportant things, but it adds up to self-protection—protection from being known.

I have never been good at lying—never smooth. In my thirties I got caught in a big lie about myself. A crisis led me there: My heart was broken, and I really didn't think I would survive. A man I had trusted had misused me, and I found myself wondering how on earth I had come to this place. How did I allow this to happen? I went through months of self-pity. My friends became frustrated that I wasn't moving on fast enough, but I had hit a wall, and God was silent.

Somewhere in that painful experience I came to a place of reckoning. When God starts taking off the glasses, you start seeing the sin in your own life, and it's a hundred times more humiliating than waking your parents up at three in the morning in a tearful confession that you were the one who put blue paint on Mrs. Peterson's white siding. I began to move on, a huge step closer to real relationships in which my self-protection could be replaced with trust. As I pursued honesty in my own life, I began to meet more people who could be trusted, who were vulnerable and transparent and honest with themselves. The lifelines in my marriage began with the ones I had already forged in myself.

Pat and I have a saying, which I tell him every morning as he is leaving: "I love you, babe, I've got your back." What I mean by that is "you can count on me to always look for the best for you and in you." It means no matter what the day brings, I am on your side. It means I'll always try to listen to you. I'll do what I can to help you see the good in each day. It's more than a catchy phrase or a romantic sentiment; it means I am on guard, praying for you and for God's protection against anything that would harm you, whether it is a career that is a dead end for your heart, or words of condemnation from a boss, or a particularly needy coworker. It means I will consciously say good things about you behind your back; I will keep your secrets and your private fears safe. It means I am your lifeline, honey, so when life gets tough, just hang on to me.

This kind of trust is only possible when two people have been relatively honest with themselves, because knowing who you can trust is a much bigger issue than finding a husband. It begins with trust in God. Only because of him can we risk being honest, authentic, and trustworthy—even when we are tempted to manipulate or fit in to be loved.

The lifeline between us is solid, but I can feel the tension on it some days. Recently I told my husband that I needed him to take over the discipline of the kids. He is like so many husbands in high-stress, high-tech jobs who seemingly go into a coma when they come home. One day I woke up and realized my eye was beginning to twitch—something had to give. I had to be honest: The problem is that for the most part I have seemed so good at handling it all. I risked looking less like Mary Poppins and more like me—who could sometimes use a sedative.

My husband's eyes used to light up whenever we talked about his dream of being a barbeque caterer. I have nightmares about standing in the tiny window of a catering truck taking orders for beef brisket, baby backs, and sweet potato pie from people with toothpicks in their teeth. But the important thing is that my husband trusts that I will never sabotage his dreams because they don't line up with mine. I realize I have power in his life. A word from me can condemn an entrepreneurial idea or fuel its fire. I choose the latter because I want a husband who doesn't settle for the status quo. I want to keep and guard the essence of who he is and what God made him for.

So every day our trust overwhelms our reasons for hiding from each other, and another thread is added to the lifeline; it's the kind of setup that only a God bigger than the universe could have thought of. In my drawer, held together with a single satin ribbon, are the first cards my husband sent me. They are precious, but more precious still are the words spoken by him just the other night: "Kathy, thank you for believing in me." "I got your back, babe," was my reply. And I do.

I hear P31 in my head; she is singing while she weaves. It is a love song, and God wrote the words. It is about what a man and a woman can accomplish when there is trust—when their lifeline keeps them tied together, keeps them buoyant. God calls this trust a model for his church. It's a sign that at the center of our relationships, God calls us into honesty and the kind of love that doesn't come in a greeting card. P31 gets out a scarlet thread that gleams in the lamplight and waxes the end as she threads it in the spindle. She weaves with great care, counting as she moves down, under, and up. She is humming as the wick shrinks and the lamp grows dimmer—the intricate fabric begins to take shape, the pattern becoming more distinct, held together by fragile threads whose strength comes from the eyes of the artist. They are honest eyes, the kind that unravel you long before the words can come. She is a woman you can trust, and as she weaves you can see what a thing of beauty comes when one thread is laid upon another until at last the tapestry is finished.

12

FIRST LIGHT

Lessons in Hope

Her arms are strong

We are not powerless specks of dust drifting around in the wind, blown by random destiny. We are, each of us, like beautiful snowflakes that God has created. There are no two snowflakes alike in the universe—not even identical twins. Each one of us is born for a specific reason and purpose.

ELIZABETH KUBLER-ROSS,
TO LIVE UNTIL WE SAY GOODBYE

It was 5:00 a.m. as Pat and I drove into the Pelican Pub parking lot to meet Joe, the owner of the Haystack Fishing Club charter service. Suddenly a truck with a rusty bottom pulled in out of the morning mist with our dory boat on a trailer behind it. The truck was affectionately named "Cream Puff," its name painted proudly in large letters on the side. Joe got out of the truck in shorts, a windbreaker, and bare feet. It couldn't have been more than forty degrees there by the looming rock of Cape Kiwanda. I was wearing several layers of sweaters and coats.

We had dreamed for a year of getting to fish on a dory boat. Dory boats are optimal for fishing because they are able to launch and be fishing in deep water in ten minutes. Most fishing was finished by noon. Joe had people booked back to back for months. We had watched them launch with the grace of a ballet company and return like a Marine landing craft beaching on the coast of Normandy. The trailer and truck operators had learned their skills from generations of dory men and women before them. We would spend hours watching for their return so that we could get a peek at their catch.

Pat and I eagerly scrambled into the boat, and Joe hauled us from one great spot to another. By the time the mist had burned off, we each had caught twenty sea bass, and we were angling for a nice ling cod. Joe told us this was sort of an "off" morning for him. Truth be told, he was a bit testy, but it was obvious that there, smoking a cigar in his bare feet, Hawaiian shirt, and shorts, Joe was doing exactly what he was born to do. The look of joy on his face was so tangible, Pat and I wanted to put it in our pocket as an example of how a person feels when they are sailing right in the groove that God has designed for them—when even on a bad day you are having so much fun you can't believe someone is actually willing to pay you for the ride.

Pat and I want to feel that way every day. Our goal in life is to have as much fun as we can. It is our belief that "real fun" is to be in exactly the place God has called us to be. Every time we see someone having fun, Pat remarks, "Do you think that guy enjoys what he does?" It is his way of saying, "See, there is another person who gets it." When you are in God's groove, you cannot hide your joy. You are a visual reminder to everyone around you that you are tapped into your calling and that not to be so would mean a slow and decaying form of emotional and soul death.

We are living in an age of great dissatisfaction. Many people are unhappy or bored with their jobs. They loathe the trap of being somewhere they were never meant to be, performing a task they find meaningless and empty. The rewards can never be enough. There is not enough money or power in the world to replace the satisfaction of hands that are busy in God's groove. There aren't enough perks to replace the feeling you get at the end of the day and the expectation of the next morning.

For the last twenty years, people in leadership have been telling us that the tide has changed. No more should we have to work a job just for money. We have choices, career counselors, change agents, and a truckload of books written on the subject.

Recently I found a web site called Road Trip Nation chronicling the tales of two Pepperdine University students named Mike and Nathan. They traveled all over the nation interviewing successful entrepreneurs to find out how they became successful. The feelings that got them started on this endeavor are familiar to many of us.

"In 1999, Mike and Nathan began questioning if they were really on the right roads. Mike, who was pursuing a career as a doctor, hated hospitals, and Nathan would nearly choke to death if he had to wear a tie. They found themselves stuck, because they didn't know what else was out there. All they had known were the standard 'roads'—doctor, accountant, and consultant—roads that didn't fit them at all."

It's an inspirational story even if you aren't twenty and don't own a Volkswagen van. Mike and Nathan bravely asked the question "what if?" "What if we could take a road trip across the entire country in an RV and take leaders from all different roads out to lunch—just to see how they got to where they are today?" Of course the bigger goal is to encourage a generation to seek their own roads, affirming my belief that the best jobs in life always have a much bigger agenda and can be referred to as a calling.

If I were going to take a road trip to talk to entrepreneurs, my first stop would be at P31's doorstep. I would ask her what helped her get there. What served as a reminder of her central purpose in life, a motivator so that she had a buoyancy tool during life's high points and rough spots and a constantly clarifying filter for her choices? I believe she found what gave her joy in her work and that "her hands were busy" doing what God had forged in her. I believe she was operating in God's groove.

I have always been struck by the fact that when Jesus met the disciples fishing by the Sea of Galilee, he didn't exchange small talk. His first words were, "I see you are fishermen. If you follow me, I'll use your skills to do something with a much bigger vision—I'll make your mission statement 'to be fishers of men.'" This is a great example of how God uses all our gifts and talents to give us a bigger agenda—the calling and purpose he has written in our souls.

I have been fortunate to have many fun and incredibly satisfying jobs in my life, but I also have always known that I had a mission that went beyond a "job." Ten years ago I wrote out a personal mission statement that has drastically changed the way I see myself and the flux and flow of kids and marriage.

Mission statements are not just for corporations and organizations. They are useful for marriages, families, and individuals. A successful mission statement represents not what you hope to become or how you hope to operate but how you naturally function, without thinking. Remember those sci-fi movies where the alien intruder's first words are, "I bring you peace"? That's his mission. He is going to do that regardless of what he gets paid, where he goes, or how many people try to kill him. A mission is something that you do regardless of your circumstances.

A mission statement expresses simply in one sentence why you are here. What is your calling? Done well, your personal mission statement also reflects the purpose for which you were born. It is the starting point for reinvention. Writing your own mission statement is a must for anyone seeking definition and clarity of their values and motivations. It is the thread of tangible hope and happiness for those of us who don't necessarily see motherhood or any other role as our whole vocation.

One of the great advantages of my mission statement is that it simplifies my life. When I'm asked to do things that don't fit my mission, it's much easier to say no. I'm not saying no because I don't want to help, but because I have limited time and energies and God wants me to be wise in my choices. One of the greatest obstacles to happiness is overextending yourself or spreading yourself too thin in the name of ministry. Having a mission statement in your pocket helps you filter your options.

When I'm scrubbing floors or doing laundry for the zillionth time, I can say to myself, *This is just for now; I have a mission that is much larger than this.* I call my mission statement my "trap door," because it reminds me that I have an escape, that I'm on my way to something larger, better, and more satisfying.

If you've tried to develop a personal mission statement before, you already know that thinking it through and writing it out are tough. I started with a list of my spiritual gifts, my talents, and things I love to do. I then made a list of ten things I have done in my life that gave me joy. I started looking for common threads in all this material to lead me in at least the general direction of "the road."

It is important to note that mission statements change with the flux of life, but the intent remains the same. Whether I am an artist or a writer, a change of medium does not change what I am. My spiritual gifts are faith, wisdom, and exhortation whether I am a camp counselor, a pastor, or a toilet cleaner. How I function in the world stays the same. What I know about myself is that I will always look for the glass half full, I will always look for the deeper meaning, and no matter where I am, I will be attempting to get others to do the same. It is my calling to do this, and I do it without thinking about it or being paid for it.

One of my earliest memories is of how I functioned in a hospital waiting room at six years old. The room was filled with other families with small children. I had been given an entire pack of LifeSavers candies. I'll never forget the feeling of going around the room and giving each child one of my LifeSavers, knowing that in that cold, inhospitable environment I had made someone smile. I don't remember eating a LifeSaver—I remember giving them away. Exhortation—standing beside and encouraging others in need—is at the core of my mission statement.

My daughter has a gift with children; she can stop a baby from crying and make whole rooms of children follow her every move. She has a gift of compassion that is always in motion, whether toward animals or people. It seeps out of her pores as she lends her listening ear, her tears, and her understanding to everyone and everything around her. If you watch anyone long enough, their core mission will be as apparent as their eye color. This is why we can benefit from getting feedback from others like family and friends. It's sometimes hard to see what is right in front of our faces.

A mission statement doesn't stop at revealing our core. It goes on to unravel the how and why of what we do. If you only have the core of your statement, you could quickly be serving on every committee known to womankind or working in a job that doesn't quite hit the mark. Your statement also needs to give some direction on how your core is best expressed. The layers of your uniqueness will need to be discovered.

So when you put your mission statement together, it might look like this: "To exhort what's true and beautiful in the ordinary and to inspire and motivate women through the use of my writing, my art, and my friendship." Or it might look like the mission statement for my family's ministry: "To give hope to the poor, homeless, and helpless through the gift of hospitality."

When people ask me to serve on a committee, I use my mission statement as a kind of filter. When Pat and I were asked to serve on a committee to help build homes for the less privileged, we offered to cook for the crew. This is how a mission statement works. It assures me of a clearer, cleaner sense of purpose in my life, serving in ways that bring me joy because I'm operating in God's groove.

Mission statements serve to define ways to best use your time and talents in ministry at church, a career change, or starting a business. They help us see our life as a giant continuum that flows into eternity. It's like switching a light on and finally seeing how God made you and for what. I have always believed that work is a form of worship and that God smiles when he sees us joyously working in the mission he gave us. I think he may even dance when he sees us finally get it—finally understand that we weren't just supposed to collect a paycheck and trudge on toward retirement. And we are at our most powerful, our most lovely, and our most purposeful when we walk with the poise and confidence of a woman who knows why she is here.

I think P31 got it. She understood that you first find what you love and look at how you were made, and then blessings will follow. She knew that together the layers of her individuality and the purpose that God had fashioned for her were powerful tools she could harness and use every day of her life. She knew this blessing of God would make the work of her hands beautiful and significant.

Nothing is more powerful than a person working in God's groove. It shows in their face, their walk, and the way they hold themselves. They are the promise to us all that even on a bad day, we can be having so much fun we won't believe that someone is actually willing to pay us for the ride.

13

SIRENS

Lessons in Passing It On

Instruction is on her tongue

I am so grateful that you have come.
I will pour out everything inside me so you
    may leave this table satisfied and fortified.
Blessings on your eyes. Blessings on your children.
Blessings on the ground beneath you.
My heart is a ladle of sweet water, brimming over.
Selah.

ANITA DIAMANT, *THE RED TENT*

THE SAILING HAD been hard, and we all were exhausted. Even in the harbor the winds continued to assault us and the waves were short and choppy. That night as I lay in my sleeping bag, the water rocked the hull below us in a steady rhythm. The storm whistled shrill in the distance.

On deck the wind began to sing, sad and mournful, as it strummed the shrouds on the mast. If I close my eyes, I can hear it still. The sound started out slow, hesitant, soft—the melody smooth, like a woman singing the blues. I closed my eyes, feeling it, being soothed by it. Then the wind grabbed the song and hit a high pitch, reverberating down into the bones of the boat. In the blackness the bitter song mingled with the sweet, and the truth of it came pouring out. It is the music of sirens, the sound of many women singing me their stories.

Women are instinctively sirens, telling our stories, sharing our knowledge and traditions. A woman shares what she knows by telling of her experiences. We carry file cabinets of information in our heads, useful information on the most effective way to treat colds and flus and remove ballpoint pen ink. Some of us pass recipe cards or endless sets of photos. Still others tell stories as we pass on carefully stitched pillowcases and quilts, the handiwork of another generation. Although we carry our lives in our purses and Daytimers, ready to exchange information, a lot of us forget that the most important information we have to pass on is not in our purse. It is the stuff of life that we are reluctant to share because we might look foolish or stupid or just bad. Yet I feel this is exactly the job of a siren—to sing her song, regardless of her imperfections. She trusts that even though her pitch may be imperfect, the melody complex, she has something of great worth to pass on. The truth is that there is much at stake. A siren sings not for herself but to help those who are desperately looking for the shoreline.

A siren is a mentor, a friend, an influencer. She is someone who touches your life, altering your perspective—giving you hope that this life can be done. The most important aspect of her life is that she is willing to risk the truth. Too many of us have not been honest. Recently on *Oprah* a new mother said it all: "Women have been sold this picture of motherhood as this gauzy, pink, warm experience, but the truth is that it's hard and lonely and sometimes I don't feel like I can do it. . . . This picture leaves me feeling like a failure at what is supposed to be the most natural event in my life."

Too many times we keep secrets to protect ourselves, denying others the benefit of our journey. A siren must be willing to be transparent and vulnerable, taking the risk to be authentic even though it might make her look less shiny. She understands that her presence in this world can be measured not by her accomplishments but by the hope she infuses to others, one woman at a time. She wields great influence by being willing to give us the raw, honest view of a woman living out loud. This is the most essential truth about sirens. Most of us would rather listen to the honest song of a sinner than the perfect song of a saint any day. Deep down we know which one we are, and we really don't trust the other.

I have had many sirens in my life. One stands out from all the rest. At age eighty-eight, she still admits her struggles to me—trusting me to keep her secrets safe. I am still just as fascinated by her life as I was twenty-five years ago when I met her. Throughout our relationship she has remained transparent, letting me see her doubts, her pain, her sacrifice, and the prayers she has waited for—even when God was silent. Though she has no biological children, she has many daughters, and I am one. When I think of what she has given me, I am profoundly grateful. She gave me a perfect view of her life, lived imperfectly, powerfully, and with great hope. She founded and continues to support a home for women in India. Recently she sent me a video the women had put together to honor her. Women of all sizes and shapes, dressed in saris and with eyes gleaming, hold up handmade signs for their "Mama Vivianna." "Mama Vivianna" was the first woman to make Christianity look like something I wanted—something I didn't want to miss.

Some women are like the picture of the rack of lamb in a Betty Crocker cookbook. They show you what the rack of lamb looks like, but they don't tell you what to do if your rack of lamb looks different. Unfortunately, if you never see a woman living honestly, telling the truth about her deep regrets and mistakes, you might think yourself a failure or try to fill your heart in ways that are contrary to your journey. I can't help but think about women like Andrea Yates. What if someone had shown her a perfect view of her imperfect journey? What if instead of judgment and self-protection, we all started telling the truth? I am convicted every time I see a woman who has been overcome by her life. I am convicted that the world needs sirens who are not the picture in the Betty Crocker cookbook but women willing to give a detailed description of how she burned the recipe.

Being a siren is like showing another woman the map of your world. Most likely the conversation will be about the obstacles on your path, not the destination. I am reminded of the Lewis and Clark journals, filled with stories of Indians and weather, bears and mountain lions. Imagine those same journals without the times of fear and uncertainty. Imagine a journal that was just a map of places. A siren takes calculated risks, understanding the value of going beyond the horizon of the known and coming back to report what she has discovered. Sirens change the world because they understand they are leaders with potential for a larger impact. They know that they are larger than their containers and that the benefits of their journey will travel far beyond the work of their hands. A siren doesn't sing for herself but so that another may be encouraged to conquer her own traps, to live less painfully and with great hope.

Recently a young woman asked if I would be her mentor. Frankly, she is light-years ahead of what I was even cognizant of at her age. She doesn't really need to hear about my accomplishments but how I arrived here. She needs to hear about the obstacles on my path, the choices that had trapped me, and the raw places they left. I was single until I was forty-one. I remember lonely nights when I ached to be touched by another human. Loneliness is something I understand. When a woman has the guts to tell me she is lonely, I don't give her a pat on the back and refer her to a Scripture. I take it in, the whole of it—because I still remember. I tell her I know the ache, I know what it feels like to go without human touch. I know there are no easy answers, except that I have survived—I am still here, and in a moment everything can change as it did for me. This is what she needs to know.

Sirens are generous of spirit and give without motive or expectations. Whether we give time or creativity, God wants us to enter into it with joy and kindness. He showed me long ago that if I live protectively and stingily, he will give me creativity at the rate of toothpaste being squeezed from a tube. Ideas are like seeds: The more I plant, the more they come to me for planting. I am no longer a tightfisted gatekeeper of my creativity or my time. I love to brainstorm, to share ideas knowing that they will return to me tenfold. The great joy of being a siren is not in having the best idea but in being a part of the process of planting seeds.

At times a siren is called upon to give opinions or constructive criticisms, but she never presses another woman to receive her guidance or advice. I have to bite my tongue when moms tell me about the blissfully close relationship they share with their eleven-year-old daughters. When a woman says something to me like, "Sarah tells me everything, and I can't imagine that will all change when she becomes a teenager," I want to shake her and scream, "Wake up, sister! You are in for the ride of your life!" Instead, I smile and say, "Good luck with that!" And I really do wish her the best, because I know it's a little like addressing the troops before they go off to war. You just don't say things like "Some of you will not survive." As a siren, I serve only as a gate to valuable resources, knowledge, and wisdom, because I am not God. I can only go where I am invited, because I am not God. I never judge or condemn or attempt to save, because once again, I am not God. The revelation is that it is enough just to be available, willing to listen, willing to ask good questions that equip a woman to discover her own solutions.

One afternoon I got a call from a friend. "I can't do this anymore. I can't live here in this" was all she said. "This" was dealing with pornography; her husband was a sex addict. "Okay," I said, "what do you want to do?" Jesus often approached people with a question. To the woman at the well he asked, "Will you give me a drink?" (John 4:7). What followed was a conversation in which the woman revealed startling facts about herself. She was a Samaritan, married five times and currently living out of wedlock. Jesus said to her, "You are right when you say you have no husband. The fact is, you have had five husbands, and the man you now have is not your husband" (John 4:18). She left her water jar, went back to the town, and said to the people, "Come, see a man who told me everything I ever did" (John 4:29). Jesus never judged this woman; instead he let the women reveal her own

145

heart and the burden she carried. He shows us that sometimes a simple question can save a life.

"You seem to have a good relationship with God, Kathy. Would you share with the group?" I was speechless. I realized that although I had attended church every Sunday of my life, been baptized with full immersion, and had, with great reluctance, given up candy for Lent—I had nothing to say. With that one question my youth group leader had unraveled me. I accepted Christ as my Savior that night. I remember that someone washed my feet to commemorate the event. Two years ago the youth leader who led me to Christ began attending my church, and I had a chance to thank him for asking me that question. Sometimes the very best advice is not going to come from you, the siren, but from the answers to your questions. A siren is always looking to expose what is good and true to those she is mentoring, and she does this with great respect and God-given insight into those he has put in her path.

A siren inspires us through the freedom and ease with which she moves through her life. She dances gracefully, even when her life is not graceful. She looks for the solid ground of faith, even though her faith is shaky. She is both a vision and a promise.

My husband and I were on a train to Montana. We had been seated in the dining car next to a woman in her eighties. She was less than five feet tall and wore a gigantic straw hat covered with big yellow and burnt orange sunflowers. I remember thinking it looked like she was wearing a Hawaiian sunset on her head. Her blue eyes twinkled at us from across the table. She had traveled the world by ship and train and now lived part of the year in Montana and part in Hawaii. She reminded me of one of my favorite movie characters from the old cult classic *Harold and Maude.* Maude crashes funerals yet celebrates life with lines like "Isn't it wonderful? All around us, living things!"

The woman with the sunset on her head savored the view from our window and pointed out landmarks to us as if saying hello to old friends. She told us about her little place in Montana and her life in Hawaii. It was obvious to us that she was still deeply in love with her husband, who had left this earthly adventure without her. After dinner she ate the chocolate mousse tart dessert with great relish, licking the spoon, making smacking noises of appreciation. When I offered her my dessert, her eyes lit up. It was fun to be in the presence of someone so free and so full of life. She said that her existence was a simple one, and yet she was a complex set of facts and figures, and as she shared her stories with us, it became apparent that she was just as fascinated with her journey as we were.

Her hat filled with flowers hinted at the untamed mission God had placed inside her. Her parting words to us were, "Don't lose your enthusiasm for life." I considered it a siren's blessing. My husband turned to me later and said, "Will you wear flowered hats when you are eighty?" I laughed, thinking how surprising, the things he knows without explanation. "Yes," I said. "Yes, I do think there is a flowered hat in my future."

Someday I may wear a Hawaiian sunset on my head. Like P31, I will have many careers and accomplish many things that will surprise even me. The purpose of my life will not be in the work but in the whole story that is my song.

P31 shows us that her song is the song of a siren as she reaches out to her sisters with words of wisdom. Her wisdom is from God and a life lived honestly. She listens to the woman who cries out, "I can't do this anymore." She sings back with kindness, soft and smooth.

God calls us to be this kind of siren. None of us can do this by ourselves. Among us are sirens and sisters looking for the shore. We are here so that they know they aren't alone. We've all stood in the blackness listening for a voice we can trust. If I close my eyes, I can hear that high-pitched song that reverberates down to my very bones. I recognize the tune—it is the music of God's sirens.

14

TIDES

Lessons in Sequencing

She considers a field and buys it

They are ill discoverers that think there is no land, when they can see nothing but sea.

SIR FRANCIS BACON, *THE ADVANCEMENT OF LEARNING*

At 8:00 a.m. on the Oregon coast, I was one of the first up in the house my family had rented for the week. As I headed toward the espresso bar across from the beach for a *breve latte,* I was struck by the low morning mist in the empty parking lot. I surrendered to the quiet and slid onto a log, drink in hand, to begin the day—to let my eyes adjust to the beach, which was also just waking.

The tide was out, exposing starfish and mussels clinging to the rocks like nursing children. A few surfers in wet suits began to dot the shore, ready for the first waves of the morning; the dory boats had been out fishing for hours, their trailers and rusted trucks parked neatly in a long row up the beach. A tour boat full of whale watchers sliced through the water on the horizon.

As I sat there watching the increasing activity, I noticed the tide changing. By the time I finished my coffee, the water line had begun covering rocks and marine gardens, washing away the morning fog and calling in the first of the fishing boats. My view had changed with it—dramatically. I moved on to meet my friends for breakfast, thinking how the tides in my own life had brought me to this place and would one day take me out again to unknown landscapes.

Is this what the Proverbs 31 woman experienced in her life? Surely she didn't do all that the Scriptures attribute to her right from the start of her life. Maybe she was a home manager and then a businesswoman, a mom and then an artist.

How different was her life from mine, from previous generations?

Our mothers' moms had one career over a lifetime. They were mothers and wives, with career options like being a secretary or a librarian.

My generation has been incredibly fortunate to have many more choices. Some of my friends left the workplace to become stay-at-home moms, and others transitioned back into the workplace as their children became less dependent on them. Our time seems more fertile than ever for a woman to reinvent herself—to have several careers and different models of "home life." Today we run cottage industries from our homes and become the CEOs of companies.

Debbie Fields was a young mother with no business experience when she opened her first cookie store in 1977. They told her she was crazy. No business could survive just selling cookies. Today Mrs. Fields is a multimillion-dollar dessert and snack empire with more than nine hundred franchised stores in the United States and eleven countries. Mary Kay Ash was a young mother who founded a cosmetics company based on principles and values straight out of Sunday school. Mary Kay is now a $1.6 billion cosmetics business with a sales force of over one million independent beauty consultants in more than thirty markets worldwide.

More recently, the brainchild of two moms provides working moms a kitchen to prepare a month's worth of meals in the time it generally takes to grocery shop. With "Dream Dinners," cofounders Stephanie Firchau and Tina Kuna believe they are giving time back to busy moms while helping them reclaim the tradition of family mealtime.

The tide is constantly changing. We live in a day and age of life coaches and change agents that help us transition, help us reinvent ourselves. We have resources for mothers transitioning into the workplace and women moving out. We have web sites like Mothers and More: The Network for Sequencing Women who help us live out the concept of "sequencing." This term was first coined by Arlene Rossen Cardozo in her 1986 book *Sequencing and Women at Home.* Cardozo refers to the mothers who move in and out of paid employment and use a variety of flexible work arrangements in order to successfully balance their work and family responsibilities.

This term is incredible powerful to me, because it leaves the door and windows in my life open for change and opportunity. It invites me to think outside the box. To date I've had four separate careers, including that of mom, and I am not finished yet. Most of my friends are now in the process of transitioning to something else; their families are at a point where they are not as dependent on them, so these women are opening up their minds to new possibilities. Others are preparing for the time when they may be able to make changes by assessing themselves, keeping journals, getting counseling, furthering their education, or being mentored by other women.

About three years ago I explored the idea of going to seminary and getting a counseling degree. When I was really honest, I realized this wasn't the best fit—the job requirements would miss whole pieces of my overall mission statement—so I let it go. I hoped around some next corner would be another opportunity.

It was looking for the next step, that passionate purpose that was just the right combination of talent and mission. I just wasn't seeing it yet.

In order to be a sequencing woman, we need to know who we are and what we want from the next step.

Two and a half years ago, driven by the madness of dust bunnies and Swiffer wet mop fumes, I offered my brainstorming expertise to a friend who worked in a design firm in Portland. He was on overload with projects and needed someone to bounce around ideas with him. I agreed to meet at his office one day, thinking this would be a chance to get out my somewhat-rusty skills and help concept a few book covers. All it took was one hour for me to realize that I had tapped into something I'd never considered—a way to move to the next round of a career without having to work nine to five.

Ever since that day, I've worked as a consultant, researching photos and illustrators and brainstorming cover and book ideas. I enjoy the creative, quirky people with whom I get to work. I have reclaimed a little of the old Kathy, and after conquering my initial fear of failure, I began to see a few glimmering facets of the future.

Our great fear is that we will succeed greatly. A big part of me is terrified of living up to the potential God has for me, because it will take me out to where the shoreline will not be familiar and I will not be safe.

Writing a book is one such experience. It's like being paid to stand naked in a shopping mall. It's terrifying and humbling, but I am typing these words regardless, taking the next baby step to making it a reality.

Baby steps are big with me, especially since I saw that movie *What About Bob?* In the film Richard Dreyfuss plays a leading psychologist who finds himself reluctantly treating Bob (played by Bill Murray), a man with severe phobic tendencies. The whole movie focuses on the psychologist's just-published book, *Baby Steps.* The book is given to Bob as his psychologist heads for a long-awaited vacation. Bob reads the book and follows him, taking baby steps to leave his apartment, baby steps to get on the bus, baby steps to find where the doctor is vacationing. The movie is hilarious as it deals with both Bob's unrealistic fears and the simple idea of taking baby steps to reach a destination, overcome a fear, and accomplish a goal.

The truth is, sequencing takes baby steps, many baby steps. Some of us will have to take baby steps just to ask, "What do I want to do next?" Some of us will need help to get there.

I feel very fortunate to have women in my circles who are natural sequencers and a husband who thinks I can do pretty much anything. I realize some of us don't have that kind of cheering section and will need to create it for ourselves. We can find courage and motivation in whatever inspires us: other women, certain groups, meditation on God's Word and ways, trips to an art gallery, journaling, books or films, or the class schedule from the local community college.

The first step is just to try on ideas—and to dream. We need to step out of the safety in our heads before we will see movement in our lives. We need to take a baby step out of the tapes and boundaries we and others have set for us, asking "what if?" and "why not?" and refusing to listen to enemy propaganda.

We need to "speak the thing" out loud. Sometimes this alone can propel us into action, but most of us need someone to speak to in order to get the momentum going.

Three years ago when I told my mother I was going to write a book, I spoke the thing out loud. Speaking a dream is like setting it in motion, because it is a prayer, and the prayer goes out and God carries it like little seeds to be sprinkled along your path. The seeds take root, and one day you realize you are standing by an oak tree and the seed came from God's blessing on your words. These words of faith are like children who grow under the shade of your protection until one day they can stand on their own.

Of course I kept thinking, *How are you going to write a book? You have nothing to say. Wait until your kids have all grown up and become rocket scientists and brain surgeons, and then maybe you'll have something to offer.* Still, I had said the thing and not to just anyone but to my mother, who has the memory of a

155

time machine. It reminded me of the advice I give to friends who lament that they want to travel but never seem to have the funds: "Buy the plane ticket." The rest will follow. And it's true: If we don't invest a baby step, we won't be able to take the leap to the next opportunity.

In the sequencing journey I've learned never to take my limitations too seriously. When I was thirty-three, I worked as art director for *Christian Parenting* magazine. When I took the job the magazine was a year old, and I was hired to produce a sixty-four-page publication. But my first issue was well over one hundred pages. I was completely overwhelmed. I remember going to my new boss and telling him that he had made a tragic error in hiring me, because this was clearly over my head. His response to me has defined my life ever since. "I know you feel like you can't do this," he said, "but that has nothing to do with what you are capable of."

It was not the last time I would feel overwhelmed, but I learned never to discount an opportunity because of what I thought I could do. Instead I operate as if I can do it until proven otherwise.

This is perhaps the most wonderful aspect of sequencing: We cannot lose. We are all traveling to an undiscovered horizon, unless we refuse to get in the boat. We will all get there in time. I remind myself of this with this thought from the late Erma Bombeck, who once said in a speech, "When I stand before God at the end of my life, I would hope that I would not have a single bit of talent left and could say, 'I used everything you gave me.'"

I believe there is great joy in using our talents—which is what sequencing involves—and that using our God-given affinities and abilities is a form of worship.

P31 must have known this. She must have sensed in all she did over a lifetime that ever-trying and -doing and -becoming make God abundantly happy, and that it is an amazing gift to be able to choose our next steps, to try on talents and walk about in them. She is a clear example of a woman who knew how to sequence her life, knew how to use every bit of magic in her fingers and every ounce of mojo in her soul. Somewhere between the lines about the supermodel of Scripture and in the life of the real woman she was, I think we miss that about P31.

A year ago Andrea decided she wanted to attend an arts academy in the area. The screening process was tough, and frankly, it seemed like a long shot. Andrea had not shown interest in the arts in the past, but in the last year she had begun to write poetry and thought she might want to go into acting. I kept thinking of the kids she was competing with for a spot—kids who had been drawing freehand since they were four, professional child actors, and agile, swan-like girls who seemed to have emerged from the womb in a leotard.

Andrea didn't seem to consider these obstacles serious. She carefully filled out the paperwork, wrote three essays, and prepared for the interview. If anyone asked her where she was going to school, she would say, "I'm going to Art and Communications Academy."

I tried to make sure she was taking a healthy approach to this and not setting up herself for disappointment. "What's Plan B?" I asked her.

"What do you mean?" she asked, shocked.

I explained that a Plan B didn't mean she had to give up on Plan A—that a backup plan just meant that she accepted all kinds of opportunities out there, and this one was just . . . one.

The idea only made Andrea more resolved to Plan A.

The day of the interview came, and after a new outfit, much pep talk and self-talk, and a few prayers from Mom, Andrea straightened her back and walked down the hall toward a room full of academy staff. I hovered, biting my nails and watching the clock.

When she returned she was with a school counselor, who kept winking at me. I decided she was telling me Andrea would be accepted, even though her mouth was telling us we would receive a letter in a couple weeks informing us of the staff's decision.

In four days that letter arrived. Andrea was accepted, art academy was a go.

"See," Andrea said. "See, I told you."

"I see," I said, sizing up the mojo in her. "I see a girl who knows what she is capable of."

The tide is always there, pulling us out to new horizons and strange oceans. The pull to something new is as joyful as it is scary. There may be no better illustration of this than between the lines of the description of P31 as every woman's hero. Yes, she was CEO of her own company, an accomplished artist, and a philanthropist who bought a field with her earnings and planted a vineyard. But as it is in all our lives, opportunities and accomplishments rarely present themselves without the simultaneous fear of failing and delirious joy of success.

I never had a good appreciation for what planting a vineyard meant until my husband and I were invited to visit one in its infancy. We saw what it took to clear the land and mark it for planting. I gazed out at a little piece of Tuscany, realizing the first vintage would not come for two years—two years to see if the soil was ready and the vines producing, two years to see if all your sweat would make your dream a reality. Did P31 know the grapes would come into season only after many baby steps of faith? Did she have a clue that fruit does not come easy or without pressure, time, and the watchful eye of God?

Maybe. Then again, maybe she possessed simply the willingness to move with the tides—knowing the time to dream, looking for the time to clear the land, seizing the moment to plant, and waiting for the fruit.

It is 7:00 A.M. in Beaverton, Oregon, today. I am one of the first up, armed with coffee made with seven scoops of my favorite grind to six cups water. (My motto will always be COFFEE IS NOT AN OPTION.) I turn on the computer. The morning fog has not lifted, and the neighborhood is just waking up. I slide into my chair with my drink in hand and begin to let my eyes adjust to the monitor. A dog barks, a squirrel scurries across my roof, and the talking heads on the news are already reminding me that I live in a world that is constantly changing as I find the page of this book I left off on and begin to write. I thank God that he has given me this gracious and good thing, this gift of the tides, and that he has brought me to this unknown shore. He will surely take me out again to a landscape unknown. I am ready.

15

RED SKY

Lessons in Courage

She has no fear

Courage is resistance to fear, mastery of fear, not absence of fear.

MARK TWAIN

I'm REMEMBERING A rhyme from my childhood: "Red sky at night—sailor's delight. Red sky in the morning—sailors take warning." It's a saying older than the Bible, and it came from the observations of sailors who studied how the skies moved over a 360-degree horizon.

I do not always have a 360-degree view of life. Often I shiver up topside, like the sailors of long ago, looking out to the horizon, hoping I can somehow avoid the imminent storms. I fear all kinds of storms, and my fears come in different sizes. Some are life-threatening. Others are merely anxiety-producing irritants. I can't tell you how many times I've asked God to appear in my living room and zap my fears away. So far he is a no-show.

For years I've let the mythical P31 woman stand like a Greek warrior goddess on her pedestal. P31 was fearless. I am not.

P31 could "laugh at the days to come." You could say about me, "She laughs nervously with some fear for the future." I fear that my son will become a drifter who plays guitar for bus fare or my daughter will marry some guy whose only skill is whittling. I fear looking foolish or, worse, being boring. Sometimes I lay staring at the ceiling at night thinking about what would happen if the moon exploded or some horrific calamity destroyed life as we know it. I fear that I will die before I get to live.

Advice columnist Ann Landers said she knew people like me. She received ten thousand letters daily; when asked what seemed to be the greatest common concern of people seeking advice, she said, "Without a doubt—fear."

As I write this it is clear that we are getting ready to go to war with Iraq. The nightly news shows men and women preparing themselves to make the ultimate sacrifice for their country. The reporters ask them, "Are you afraid?"

"Yes, I'm anxious, but we are prepared," they each say with only slight variation. Their young faces betray them.

Yesterday Katie Couric interviewed Evelyn Husbands, the wife of astronaut Rick Husbands who was lost in the space shuttle *Columbia* tragedy. Evelyn bravely talked about her husband's life, the loss still raw, the pain uncloaked.

Later, in my yard, I thought, *Where does this courage come from? I've been looking for it all my life.* And then I noticed our camellia tree. Every year it blooms vivid, fuchsia-colored flowers. Shortly after opening, the blooms fall to the ground like small umbrellas until the tree is completely bare, leaving the ground alive with color. It's a small, seemingly insignificant event, occurring quietly and without applause.

It reminds me that often our responses to fear are small acts of courage that only we can see, like scheduling a mammogram every year even though it makes you anxious, getting on an airplane even though you're afraid, or meeting with the school principal because your daughter called someone a name.

Courage is an "even though" response to fear. It says, Even though I'm trembling, I'll act as though I'm not.

Even though I'm afraid, I'll respond as though I'm brave. Even though that person intimidates me, I'll speak to her. It says, I will visit someone who needs me in the hospital, even though I don't know what to say. I will reach out to those who are not like me, even though it takes me out of my comfort zone.

Pat and I had only been married for two months when we made the decision to fight for custody of Andrea and Patrick. Preparing for court became a full-time job of collecting paperwork, hiring investigators, meeting with attorneys and child psychologists, and dealing with ongoing visitations that were becoming difficult and dangerous.

I thought I would break out in hives the first day of court. I have vivid memories of my mother biting her nails and handing out chunks of Hershey's to us when she was stressed out. What I wouldn't have given for a Milky Way or a package of Ding Dongs during the hearings.

My legs were visibly trembling as I was being sworn in, and I was searching for enough saliva to voice the oath and sit down. I thought of something my father told me when I was taking my driver's test: "They don't know all the stupid things you've done—they just need to know that you are safe enough to put on the road."

I repeated in my head, "You don't need to prove yourself the mother of the year, Kathy—just tell them who you are."

The first day in court rolled into the next and the next until on the fifth day we walked out to tell our kids they could pack their bags—for good—and come home to us.

Somewhere in the process, I chose to act as though I wasn't afraid. Funny thing: If you don't give fear oxygen, it evaporates before your eyes. I discovered that fear leaves when you act in a way that's contradictory to what you feel. What gives fear power, however, is hand-fidgeting, gut-churning, fist-in-your-esophagus and hot-wax-in-your-gullet obsessing.

I understand such obsession. I love to sing but for years couldn't bring myself to sing alone on stage. I obsessed over how I sounded, over being good enough. Every time I attempted a solo, my hands would get clammy, my heart would race, and my stomach would turn slowly and painfully like one of those big cement trucks. I prayed and waited for the fear to leave me, but it never did. This made me mad—so mad I decided if I died trying to overcome fear and sing to a crowd, the experience would be worth the trade. So I set a date and began to prepare for the performance. I kept telling myself I wasn't going to call in sick or find someone to replace me. I wouldn't let myself off the hook. I was doing this.

I told God, I'm willing to fail. I'm willing to look stupid on stage, and if I have a heart attack, well, that would be worth not being stuck in Fear City.

The day I got up and sang, I was eternally grateful that no one could read my mind. I was wrestling with myself all the way to the mic. A voice deep inside screamed, "Run. . . . You're going to die. . . . Now you've done it. . . . Are you crazy? . . . Don't go, don't goooo!"

I was already there and singing the first line of the song when I realized that the voices in my head had stopped screaming at me. Instead I heard, "You're doing it. . . . Knew you could. . . . I've been telling you all along that this was a piece of cake— look, they are smiling! . . . You are doing all right. . . . Isn't this fun?"

Courage is the choice we make in our heads not to run. We are plagued by memories of fearful and painful moments, like the day my pantyhose fell down around my ankles while I was delivering a science report in front of Mrs. Wolf's sixth grade class or the day I sat shivering in a blue paper gown while my doctor told me they had found a lump in my breast.

The truth is, we all are afraid. Peter was afraid to get out of the boat to meet Jesus on the water, Joseph was afraid to marry the mother of Christ, and as our Savior hung on the cross, he cried out in the human fear he felt, "My God, my God, why have you forsaken me?" (Matt. 27:46). Our greatest fear is not death but that when we take a step out from our life, God will not be there.

Long before, was P31 ever afraid? When her children ran high fevers, when her investments were risky, or when her husband was stressed out? When the times called for heroic deeds, did she make the choice to be brave?

Both of our kids perform. Patrick plays in a band, and Andrea acts and is a poet who gives readings. Recently Andrea told me she wasn't going to write poetry anymore because a few students at her school had told her that her poetry stunk.

"So write a poem about judging others' work," I suggested. "That's what courageous artists do—they respond to the fear in their lives using the very gifts the enemy wants to paralyze."

I tell my kids, "Fear is the norm. What we do with it is what makes us extraordinary."

Amazingly, my father just seems to live completely without fear. A couple of years ago I witnessed him chase a bear away from our campsite and hit it in the butt with a rock. I asked him, "What was Plan B?" He didn't answer, but I was pretty sure there wasn't one.

I remember how when I was nine he slept in front of our tent in Yellowstone with an axe in his hand after a bear had torn into the tent hours before. I remember him crawling to the highway with broken ribs to flag down help when we had been in a car accident. He always managed to make me feel safer, more protected.

My father is never more fully alive, fighting fear, than when he is sailing in foul weather. When the water kicked up like a bronco and the wind held us fast, my instinct was to head below to get out of the relentless waves that crashed over the bow and the wind that howled like a demon. I hated foul weather because it scared me. It made me imagine headlines like SPRING SAIL TURNS DEADLY—FAMILY LOST AT SEA. Bad weather just made my father put on his yellow rain gear. He would stand straight as water and waves pelted him, and he'd hold the tiller with one hand as he squinted into the horizon. Water could slosh around his feet and the salt spray could sting his face and fog his glasses, and he would be smiling still. I was both comforted and confounded to see this. Even though the winds blew and the boat rocked, he was standing there, and he was not afraid.

167

Fast forward fifteen years. I am sitting in an intensive care room. In a bed across from me, a man whom I hardly recognize is hooked up to various machines. I count the tubes running in and out of his body to monitors on his left and right. I look closely at the man's face; only traces hint at his former appearance, but I know that he is my father. I am sitting like all the others, feeling helpless, drinking hospital coffee, watching the heart monitor, and listening to the gentle hum of the machines around me. The only thing that breaks my concentration is an occasional battalion of balloons or flowers being delivered or brought to cheer the families. My stomach is cramping from the fear.

Hours before, I had asked him if he was afraid.

"I would be stupid to not be afraid," he said.

He had stunned me. Seeing my fear, he took my hand and assured me that it would be okay.

"God still has things for me to do," he comforted.

I wondered. Does God ever really let us in on when our jobs on earth are over? I struggled with how to assure him, despite the bravado, that whatever was to be was alright.

I began singing softly to the man in the bed, hoping he could hear me somewhere beneath the painkillers and anesthesia. As I sang my fear began to slip away, and something resembling courage moved through me.

The intensive care unit grew mysteriously quiet, and it seemed the typical movement of nurses checking patients or equipment being rolled away just ceased. My quiet singing had become more audible, and I wondered if I was disturbing the other families. Then I looked down at my father's face, studying him closely, and I saw tears rolling down his cheeks, each replaced with another in steady succession. I sat there singing for a long time so that he would know: *I am here even though I am afraid.*

God tells us that when we are afraid, there is work to do—and the stakes are high. An enemy is at the door and seeks to paralyze you, tie you up in knots, and ultimately destroy you. But God, on the other hand, wants you to see that you are brave, that you have a choice.

Our heavenly Father redeems the most fearful of moments to us when we choose to walk straight for them instead of running in panic. I think of the tragic disasters of 9/11 and the moments that followed. They gave us stories of heroism, of strength and tenacity of spirit, and yet no doubt many were trembling in those horrific minutes. They were fathers and brothers and moms like me, who clung to the courage that God had revealed to them over a lifetime. In those seconds that became hours, they most likely wondered where God was. Perhaps the answer to that question was what helped them climb those stairs to reach others or help someone down the endless flights to safety.

My husband spent twelve years as a firefighter. Because I am his wife, I know the name of every fire truck in our area. Our kids can identify them by the sound of their sirens. Sometimes we chase them. My husband loves the fire service but can no longer serve because of a chronic cough.

Many times in his fire career, Pat had reason to fear, but one in particular stands as the defining moment of his career. At age two Andrea had open-heart surgery, and he had almost lost her. The stress had overwhelmed him. His nerves were shot, and he began to doubt his ability to fight fires. He was still doing odd jobs around the firehouse and staying in shape at the gym, but he found himself not wanting to be there when the alarm sounded.

One day he was at the gym when his pager went off. He drove to the firehouse thinking he could help out. When he arrived he was met by the chief, who told him to grab his turnouts and get in the truck. The Chevy Blazer was clocking 85 miles per hour all the way to the fire. It was a restaurant, and Pat and the chief were the first on the scene. Flames had licked through the roof, turning the sky black. The chief told Pat to put on his breathing apparatus; he would be the first in the building.

Pat stood there waiting for the engine to arrive, sweat pouring down his back. A second man on the hose arrived. As Pat held the nozzle and hoisted hundreds of pounds of hose behind him, he walked straight into the very thing that he had come to fear.

I asked him, "When did the fear leave you?"

He answered without hesitation, "The moment I went through the front door."

I've been looking for courage all my life, and yet in life I believe it is our everyday choices to be brave that stretch from our kitchens out into our world. I believe P31 refused to be paralyzed by fear in her life, that she summoned courage to reach out to her community, to be led into places that were not safe, and to stretch. She had an attitude of confidence that

God would never leave her. She clung to the part of her that refused to be ruled by her anxiety and concerns. She stood in the middle of her life without a 360-degree view of the horizon. Even though red covered her sliver of sky, she chose courage, though she may have been trembling.

The fact is, we all tremble, and we are all brave. God calls bravery forth from our lives so he can say, "See, I knew you had it in you."

Though the voices in our head are screaming in panic, he whispers, "Stay. Resist. Fight. See what happens. If you do, the prize is life and freedom and your way back to the center." It is also the knowledge that fear evaporates in the midst of courage and that even when the world isn't looking, you will become like a camellia tree in spring.

16

SUN CATCHER

Lessons in Laughter

Her children . . . call her blessed

Getting there isn't half the fun—it's all the fun.

ROBERT TOWNSEND

The kite shop was ablaze with color, from pink and turquoise to red and yellow. Giant sails of fabric swathed the ceiling in shapes of birds, whales, and flowers. Sun catchers glinted in windows—circles of glass in a rainbow of colors. As I walked from one room to the next in search of the world's most perfect kite, the effect dazzled me and dizzied me.

A small girl dressed in a fairy costume ran up to the biggest kite in the shop. She was about five years old with hair that looked like a red Brillo pad. Her father was close in tow. Embracing the huge purple and black Keiko kite that mimicked the famous whale, the girl beamed, "I'll fly this one." Then, pointing to a rather small pink kite in the corner, she announced, "You can fly that one, Daddy."

The look on the father's face was so transparent, I started to laugh. I visualized the huge kite being towed to the beach by the tiny fairy princess and her giant father faithfully marching behind with the miniature pink starter kite. It was the extravagance, the over-the-top quality of that picture that made me laugh—out loud, and not quietly. The sound went clear through me, vibrating down my sides, bringing tears to my eyes, bubbling out.

I love to laugh, and I laugh frequently and loudly. My kids won't sit with me in theaters, and some of my friends (not the good ones) sometimes shush me. But I like the sound that goes right through me, the way I cannot contain it—I don't think any of us should.

It's a good thing, laughter, because reality isn't always extravagant or generous or funny, and reality is where moms live. There are so many things about parenting in general that can make you crazy, and sometimes laughter is the only weapon you have to keep from committing yourself.

Right now my son is in the throes of what the experts are now calling "the launching years." It's a term that describes eighteen- to twenty-four-year-olds in transition from being a teenager to becoming an adult. So far I rate it up there with a colonoscopy or being treated with leeches. I pray that by the time this book is published, something gets launched. Until then there are worries and there is angst, the kind that can consume you. If you can't laugh, the whole child-rearing thing seems like a death knell.

When the kids first came to live with us, I was admittedly an overachiever. My goal was to create an environment of safety, with rituals and boundaries, outlets and opportunities for healthy growth. I signed us up for art and drama workshops. I enrolled Patrick in a school to help him with his math and started Andrea on the swim team. I set up brightly colored, laminated chore checklists. I bought the kids new wardrobes, new beds, new linens, new everything. I got their teeth checked, took them to physicals, met with the principals at their prospective schools. By the end of the summer I was exhausted, and the kids just watched in wonder as this crazy lady knocked herself out.

Laughter saved us when all these best intentions were marred by too much reality—by burnt dinners and crabbiness, too much homework and sheer exhaustion.

I quickly learned that my kids will forget every perfect meal I ever cooked. They have already forgotten what they ate last night. What they tend to remember are the events and times in our lives that were less than perfect and how we reacted.

The Christmas Pat fixed a beautiful piece of prime rib, he waited in the bakery line two hours for the perfect complementary potato rolls. When dinnertime came, we passed around those perfect rolls and dug into the feast that had been so carefully prepared. What my kids remember is not the dinner, the beautiful decorations, the warm lights, and the stunning tree. What they find memorable about that Christmas is that in the middle of the dinner the dog walked up to the perfect potato rolls sitting in a basket on the floor, lifted his leg, and . . . the rest is not pretty, but it is family history all the same.

Laughter holds that history like it holds other turning points for us. Turning points like when Pat and I despaired that Patrick would wear nothing but black, draw only pictures of death and skulls, and listen constantly to music that sounded like a headbanger's funeral liturgy. We were concerned. Then I began to notice that every time Patrick tried to be really dark and rebellious, his own little light would foil him. It's hard to look tough when you have dimples the size of golf balls on your face. So we learned to look past the black for the light.

One day Patrick bought a long black trench coat from Goodwill and decorated it with a hundred silver studs. This was post-Columbine, and parents feared the signs of anything related to the tragedy: their sons playing too many video games or wanting to wear a trench coat to school. Upon closer inspection of the coat, though, I began to feel there was something not-so-sinister here; something was "off." As my son proudly modeled his new creation, he spun around to give us the full effect—and there it was, the thing I couldn't put my finger on at first. The back of his menacing black trench coat revealed a feminine scalloped design. I couldn't help but laugh, and Patrick soon joined me. He had mistakenly bought a woman's coat.

If I can't find levity somewhere in the mix, some joy and humor in their everyday antics, then truly I am lost.

Is this what P31 taught her children—that you laugh not because things are easy but because things often work out differently than you expect or because mistakes are made? Did P31 find the irony of life funny? Did she understand that wisdom is not in being flawlessly prepared, but instead the reward is in the dinner or family vacation *with* an incident—and in what you make of it?

I've wondered about this more the longer I've practiced parenthood. Let's face it—I need to keep laughing so my kids can see that their mom doesn't take herself too seriously, that mistakes are no big deal, that flops in the kitchen are hilarious, and that the fly in the soup always makes a good story.

177

Besides, kids are funny. Being a mom can be funny too.

Often dinnertime at our house ends with us laughing so hard tears stream down our cheeks—not because our home mirrors the Cleavers' on TV, but more because things can be so threatening we must laugh, and in the fear or doubts find humor, and in the humor find relief.

When I first met my kids, we were all looking for ways to bond. I've long believed laughter is the medicine of my life; it releases me from the trap of taking myself too seriously and shakes me back to center. It is the way I bond with my family and friends, so I decided to play a little game. I dared the kids to look at my glass eye (which I do not have) and asked if they could tell which one it was. They guessed it was the left. Pat and I had found a key chain with a glass eye on it, so when April 1 came, my fake glass eye found its way into a bedside glass . . . and in our house April Fool's is now a holiday.

Another humorous memory involves vacations; my kids barely remember our vacation to Disneyland, but they remember our first camping trip. Their father had bought so much Coleman gear we had to rent a U-Haul trailer. Now when we see an SUV pulling a U-Haul, our kids are convinced the occupants must be going camping.

They remember the time a black bear wandered into our campsite and grabbed a whole tub of Rice Krispy treats, returning later covered in marshmallow and pine needles, looking for more. This one event inspired campfire odes, poetry, and songs and an essay from my daughter titled "Why I'm No Longer Afraid of Bees."

Laughter is my emotional sun catcher—reflecting off my joy and my cares. It often defies our circumstances, temporarily stops obsessive worry, thwarts feelings of depression and hopelessness.

Sometimes the only thing we can do is laugh.

In the days preparing for court, Pat and I were knee deep in the ugliness of investigations and psychologists' reports. We often felt overwhelmed by the awesomeness of the task. It was like we were secret agents in a foreign country and the tape detailing the secret mission had just self-destructed.

One day Pat started singing, "Secret Agent Man," complete with his own jig for accompaniment. There was my husband, dancing around the room giggling, "Secret agent man, secret agent man, they've given you a number and taken away your name. . . ."

I laughed so hard I couldn't feel my lips. The song stuck; now whenever we feel like the job of parenting is too daunting, we sing it, and sometimes we dance.

We're grateful that our kids are especially funny, and not just because they are teenagers but because they generally look for the humor in life. It is my prayer and hope that they always will, because laughter will protect them from despairing over the tough places and hard times.

Andrea has a tendency to flip around words, often changing the meaning. One of her favorite comments is, "The week has worn down on me." Our family decided that was a much better description than "The week has worn me down."

When the week has been particularly tough, my husband and I have been known to have pillow fights until our kids bang on the door and yell at us to settle down.

My kids call me "CSI Mom" because I am a keen observer of the forensic evidence of teenage behavior—after all, I was young once, although they like to remind me that it was before the invention of electricity and running water. They still don't know how I can tell when they are hiding something or how I know when they aren't telling the truth. Once I overheard my son talking to his friend about me. "You don't understand," he was saying. "We've got to tell her the truth. She does this CSI thing where she just keeps asking you questions until you can't take it anymore. It's scary."

I admit, something about being a mom brings out the forensic scientist in me. But my kids notice everything I do as well. They tease me about my morning hair, which actually does things that defy gravity. They kid me about my directional skills (none), my taste in music (all over the map), and the fact that I am rarely far from my cosmetic bag, which they refer to as Mom's Bag O' Makeup.

Humor is a gift we all come by honestly.

I grew up in a family where humor was our arsenal. My family taught me to laugh: at each other, at our stories, at our mistakes. They taught me that even in the worst times, the most painful times, there are reasons to laugh.

I remember trading wit and banter over the dinner table. My father was head comedian. He teased us without mercy and we loved it, even when he pretended our hair rollers could pick up radio stations or told us he was going to the next restaurant table to ask for a bite of their desserts. We learned that life was like a theater and we were going to get as much joy and laughter as we were willing to write into the script. We also learned to hold our faults and shortcomings loosely, and I developed a working motto: "If it's not fun, I'm not doing it."

I remember a Christmas after my father's cancer surgery. My sister and my dad were in the kitchen cooking a dish that called for precooked manicotti shells. As I walked into the kitchen, I heard them laughing uproariously. They both pointed up, where dinner hung by a noodle. They had decided that manicotti shells were *al dente* if they stuck to the ceiling. We refer to this as the Christmas with the *pasta ā la ceiling*.

My grandmother was a very serious woman who wore hats to church and was slow to give compliments. She never partied, danced, drank alcohol, or went skinny dipping in July. But when she laughed, she was shameless. It would start with a bell-like sing-song sound that seemed to originate at the top of her head and shake all the way down to her hips. It seemed contradictory to her nature, but laughter revealed what was at her core.

Like my grandmother, I am a woman whose humor resides at the center. Planted in me is a legacy of faith, optimism, and humor that bubbles up when the world traps me in a corner. It explodes out and helps me to hold the balance of things.

A relative first called my attention to the quality in my laugh. Grinning from ear to ear, she said, "Don't ever stop laughing, Kathy. It's a blessing."

181

Humor is a blessing—a personal one I pass on to my kids. It witnesses to our insides what we do not see with our eyes. That's one reason laughter is good for our emotional health, allowing us to express emotions of fear or frustration. The chemicals released in the brain make us more alert and even help us deal with pain. When we laugh, we cannot produce the hormones that cause stress. Humans are the only creatures on earth with the ability to laugh. You don't need to be a brain surgeon to know that it feels good.

I've come to realize that when life has its foot on my head, I need to seek out friends who can make me laugh. Four or five times a year, Pat and I meet our friends Aaron and Chris for a weekend of laughter and relaxation—in that order. We forget our responsibilities and the pressures and take a vacation from our worries. We eat junk food, stay up late, and laugh until we double over. In short we act like kids, because most of the time we can't.

For one of these vacations a year ago, Pat and I brought along a deck of UNO cards. We played husbands versus wives. The first several games were won by the men, who did a little victory dance. Then Chris and I named our team "The Handmaidens of God," and "The Big Dogs" haven't won a game since.

We've tapped into that strategy that I believe P31 knew— one secret to so much of her successes. It is one of the oldest, most readily available remedies to help deal with everything from launching years to cancer. It is this potent, life-giving, sensory-overloading buzz that God calls good medicine. We need to inhale it every day, grab it, make room for it in our

families, and look for it in our mistakes. Maybe it is the blessing P31 received from her children: laughter, the kind that
shook down to her hips, the sort that gave her buoyancy at
her core and created a sound that went clear through her. It
is in the unexpected blessing of motherhood, the lesson my
children teach me every day and the one I try to model for
them. I can hear P31 calling from her life: "Don't ever stop
laughing, girl—it's a blessing."

17

SIGNS

Lessons in Wisdom

She watches

You just have to ask yourself, what kind of person are you? Are you the type who sees signs? Sees miracles? Or do you think that people just get lucky? . . . Is it possible that there are no coincidences?

GRAHAM HESS IN THE FILM *SIGNS*

I PRAYED THAT God would give me a sign. I was twenty-three, working in downtown Seattle, and I felt my life was drifting. I had no particular problems, but as I left my job one afternoon and headed for the bus, I wondered what purpose I was serving.

Why am I here? I thought. No one was asking me to quote the four spiritual laws; no one seemed to want to hear about Jesus; no one wanted to be discipled by me; and I hadn't won anyone to Christ.

"Give me a sign, God," I whispered as I mounted the steps of the metro bus. Silently I wished for—needed—a glimpse of the big picture God surely had sketched out for me on a blueprint in his back pocket. I looked from one resigned face to the next at the back of the bus, then silently prayed, "I know you are bigger than this, than each of us, than me. Let me see what you see."

I glanced up at the advertisement displayed across the top of the bus—it made me take a long breath and exhale slowly. Directly across from me was a detergent ad that said . . . everything.

YOUR JOY SHOWS.

Something in me shifted. I connected with the message and left the bus feeling happy and focused and as if God had

186

positioned that at just the right time, in just the right place, just for me. I called my friends, who all seemed to agree that, no, God probably didn't speak through detergent ads, but they were glad I'd been affirmed this day.

But I saw something they didn't, and this may be the one thing about signs that God holds intimately between himself and the receiver: Only the one receiving the sign knows whether it was God or just a bus advertisement. Signs are a mystery, and God doesn't deliver mystery to those who refuse to see it.

Years later, after I had left my job, I ran into some former coworkers from the place I'd left. They embraced me.

"It's never been the same since you left," one said. Another, "It's never been as fun." And so on: "No one laughs and jokes like we used to." "It's like the joy is gone."

YOUR JOY SHOWS.

I remembered that sign, that day on the bus, God's message in a soap ad, and my friends' doubt that God speaks to us like this. I smiled and secretly thanked him for telling me what I needed to know, what made me powerful, what special mission he had for me in this world.

I knew then that we all need signs.

I'm convinced now, as a mother and wife, of the importance of the signs all around us—they are like small tremors in the earth and our lives. They signal that our marriages need help, our children are in trouble, our finances could use more management, and our spiritual walk needs to be strengthened. And beneath these tremors are also signs that God is near, that we've grown in our relationship with him, that marriages have passed through testing successfully, and that our children have finally remembered some of the valuable things we've fought so long and hard to teach them.

These signs reside in the shadows of our lives, and we must have eyes to see them and wisdom to interpret what they mean.

Signs are part of the life of God's chosen, and there is evidence that P31 heeded them. Proverbs 31 tells me she watched over the affairs of her household. She looked for signs of coming winter in the sky so she would be prepared with warm clothes. She watched the eyes of her sons and daughters for signs of well-being. She must have heard the same stories I know—of men and women who lived by signs while others around them worried for their sanity. Stories of folks like Noah, who built an ark and watched for a sign when it was time to float and when it was time to step out of the boat. But she couldn't have known the later stacks of signs in the Bible: how Joseph followed the signs to a stable for the birth of his son Jesus, how a star led three kings to Jesus' first earthly bedside, how the disciples received the sign of Pentecost after Christ's resurrection, how God has given us signs to mark Jesus' second coming, and how he will signal us again when the ultimate battle comes.

So I look for signs in my life like P31 must have looked for them in hers—in the eyes of my son and daughter, in my husband's eyes, in my mirror. The view isn't always serene.

Yesterday my son moved away from home. With all the arrogance of a nineteen-year-old, he woke up one morning to discover he knew everything. So I stood there watching him load his belongings into a U-Haul, wondering, *Will he still hear my voice and the voice of his father in his head whenever he's tempted to act as something other than a man of integrity? Will he sense our presence as he goes about his daily life? Will he stay safe and face his trials instead of running?*

I held in my arms a stuffed gorilla that I had given Patrick for Valentine's Day. *Will he ever realize how much we love him and how amazing God made him?* I thought. *Will he be able to read the signs and find his way through the windy road to his own destiny?* I questioned what kind of job I did. *Will he judge me later for my weakness as a parent or blame me for my frailties? Will he remember what I did for him? Will he value my sacrifice? Did he get it?*

When a child leaves home, it is abundantly clear that not only are we parents not in control, but any hope of further effecting change has now been eradicated. It is an obvious sign that we cannot contradict; it's a sign we can only see from a fragile place, hoping our child is ready for the elements that will test him.

Looking back, there were many signs that told us that Patrick was ready to leave—many signs over a long period of time. He had strained harder against our boundaries. He had fought more to do things his own way. There had been arguments and rebellion over hair and clothes and life philosophy.

Just as Patrick arrived to his birth mother after birthing pains, this leaving was messy. I never expected it to be easy or painless to see a child leave. I just never anticipated the pain and fear I'd feel—the fear because I know what is out there, and the pain because there were things I'd tried to buffer my children from and now couldn't, and because when our children leave us, they change not just their world but ours as well.

So Patrick left and our daughter, Andrea, got up this morning and quipped, "One down, one to go."

That one has gone must be slightly scary to the one that is left behind, but Andrea couldn't have known the double edge I felt on that sword.

I cannot deny that through our kids' teen years I've sometimes fantasized about my life once the kids are out making their own way. Pat and I have never been married without children, so parts of us dream of things like quiet dinners or finding there are still eggs and milk in the refrigerator even after days without trips to the store. But then parts of us are unsure we will like these things half as much as in our fantasies, and what would we do with all the empty rooms in the house anyway?

Today Patrick called to tell how he had grocery shopped for the first time by himself. He told me everything he had purchased, down to the last cent, and then confessed that somewhere between the ATM and the grocery store he had misplaced a twenty-dollar bill.

"You are going to make lots of mistakes," I said. "Try to be more careful next time and just move on."

"I know," he said, "but I almost took my pants off in the store trying to find that twenty."

I smiled to myself. *Yep,* I thought, *this will be good experience for the boy. It's a sign,* I thought. *He's stretching his legs. He's*

190

*living out loud and making mistakes. This is the way the road is
as you head toward your life. One day he'll realize that, and then
he'll realize he's standing on his own.*

I recognize the signs that Patrick is growing, the birthing
pains of reality, and I will try to give him the consolation of
someone who lived there once. I remember the times my own
parents bailed me out of some bounced checks, listening patiently as I preached righteously about the wrongs of stagger-
ingly high nonsufficient funds fees and banks in general. I lost
count of how many times my mother went over the importance
of balancing my checkbook and reconciling bank statements
with my own checking records. These mistakes too are signs that
a person is growing, maturing, running up against the boundaries of the real world instead of the one carefully constructed for
one's own comfort and safety.

Signs jolt us from comfort, or from comfort's destination—
complacency. Warning signs come in many sizes, from the sign
that we need to make lifestyle changes to the signs like ones
delivered to Pharaoh or to the cities of Sodom and Gomorrah.
God set the whole system in play so that if we are watching and
wise, we can respond to the warning signs in our lives before
they destroy us.

The warning signs in my own life are the first type: my body
has been gently telling me for the last three years that I need
more exercise. I'm finally responding to the warning signs of
aching knees, dwindling energy, and the need for oxygen every
time I climb four flights of stairs. Finally I'm willing to take
seriously the small voice that keeps telling me to take care of

191

myself. Of course, the root reason I'm finally listening is the many nights lately I've woken in a cold sweat of realization that if I don't act on that voice, I probably won't live past seventy. As much as I try to convince myself otherwise, walking a dog who wants to stop every few yards to smell all forms of foliage is not really cardiovascular exercise.

So yesterday at 6:00 P.M. I handed my husband a frozen dinner and left for a workout in a small women's gym near our home. The day before I had met my personal trainer and visited the store to buy workout capris, a T-shirt, and new athletic shoes, repeating to myself all the way, "This too shall pass."

Our bodies and minds are constantly telling us information we need to listen to: our cholesterol or blood pressure is high, we aren't sleeping well or enough, we've gained back our lost weight, or we can't seem to fight off infection and viruses like we used to. Our emotions may be all over the place, yo-yoing from anger to tears; we may feel tired all the time, hopeless, or full of anxiety. If we ignore the signs, parts of us start to shut down. Our bodies reach critical condition, and we get sick or can no longer function.

I watch for the warning signs in my family: I notice when my husband isn't handling the stress at work as well as he has in the past or when my daughter isn't sleeping well.

"What's going on at school?" I ask her.

Always the first response is "Nothing," and then, "You read way too much into everything—there always has to be some huge issue for you."

I stand my ground and wait for her to finish venting, because I know she will end up heaped in my arms crying as the problem she's been battling for days comes spilling out.

These are the everyday signs in my household. Are they any less great than the dramatic signs and wonders of the Bible—the burning bush Moses saw, the light that blinded Paul?

There are other signs that dazzle our minds; they are miraculous in nature and confirm in us that God is with us and he is every inch exactly who we think he is—and yet so much more. He reminds us that even when we aren't looking, his mysteries are at play in our lives.

This is what I found provocative in the movie *Signs,* where a priest grieves the loss of his wife and struggles with the seen and the unseen in keeping the faith. Set in rural Pennsylvania, this drama follows a family grappling with a hostile invasion of aliens—but this family's story is really more about how to come to terms with miracles and signs.

Take this interesting conversation in which the priest asks his brother what kind of a person he is: "Are you the type that sees signs?" he asks. "Sees miracles? Or do you think that people just get lucky?"

His point is that signs surface in the everyday life and we must choose how to identify them—as miraculous or coincidental. To others these signs may be meaningless, but to each of us who can connect up the small occurrences that led to the event, they are nothing short of wonderful, comforting realizations that God exists and is still operating in this realm.

In 1986 my father was told by his doctors that his outlook for recovery from cancer was uncertain. My parents took it as a sign that they needed to radically change their lifestyle. My mother sold her CPA practice, and my father took early retirement. They sold their condo in downtown Seattle at a loss, got on their sailboat, and sailed to Alaska. They have been having the time of their lives ever since.

The fact that my father is still around to repair roofs and dance with my mother is a miracle. He's among the 2 percent of people who survive melanoma. I well remember all the people who prayed for my dad.

My husband faced something similar—going into a small hospital chapel when two-year-old Andrea had a Strep B infection after heart surgery. When things were at their worst, he begged God for a miracle. The fact that the daughter we love survived is indeed a miracle.

Some people may call such events luck or coincidence, because God probably doesn't speak through detergent ads. But I know something in my gut, like P31: Everything happens for a reason. All of life is significant. God is alive and operational. What the doubter may scoff at as luck, P31 could know in her gut to be nothing short of the parting of the Red Sea. She used the wisdom of one who watches to interpret the small changes in her family and community. She watched, expecting she would see. P31 lived her life looking for and expecting divine intervention.

Watching like P31 has changed the way I am doing this ride called motherhood. I am learning to expect that one day I will watch my son graduate from college, play in the symphony, marry someone wonderful, and most importantly discover what God created for him and only him to do. I am watching and expecting that my daughter will come to me with her heart cries and we will sort them out together; that my body will tell me what it needs; that my husband will show me when I can encourage him most.

I am seeing that signs and wonders are a mystery—and God doesn't deliver mystery to those who refuse to see.

When I feel like I need to save the world or my children or my home, P31's example gently tells me, no, I can't save the world, and all I have to do is be Kathy, God's Kathy. God has designed signs to tell me that this drama is his, that he is here and he is every inch exactly who I think he is—that and more. In the meantime I will keep watching for him in detergent ads, in a burnished sunset sky, and in the faces of my family.

18

~~~~~~~~

RED CANOE

Lessons for the Journey

You surpass them all

And we, who with unveiled faces all reflect the Lord's glory, are being transformed into his likeness with ever-increasing glory, which comes from the Lord, who is the Spirit.

2 CORINTHIANS 3:18

THE SMALL LAKE was surrounded by soft groves of trees and pink-and-white water lilies. Its color-washed edges were interrupted by the dock that reached out like fingertips over the lake's glassy skin. Agile deer munched grass, unafraid of the occasional car that carefully observed the many signs posted to SLOW DOWN. As Pat and I pulled into the gravel parking strip in front of our cabin, I noticed the sky was filled with lazy, languid clouds. I had a special feeling for this place, a kind of familiarity that flooded my heart until I thought it was going to burst.

This wasn't just a stop along the way. This was a destination.

Within an hour I was floating on my back in the lake, squinting up at the sun, finding shapes in the clouds, fanning my arms, and smiling. I thought about my past year in small snapshots, keenly aware of the ruthlessly hard ground I'd stumbled over. Gut-shaking images flooded my mind. I had been in a place of loneliness, pain, and frustration.

What a contrast to where I lay now, in a cool envelope of water.

There were no sounds of motorboats or frenetic skiers slicing through the lake; no high-pitched commercials blaring from radios or car engines rumbling and horns honking; no timers ticking or washing machines chugging—just quietness punctuated at intervals by the faint, odd splash of children swimming . . . somewhere over there . . .

I didn't look, just floated in the water with an overwhelming sense of peace as the late summer sun warmed my face.

I began thanking God for bringing me this far and for giving me the recognition that Pat and I had arrived here intact. We would see other crises, no doubt, but this trial was done.

After a while I found myself just listening to the gurgle of the water as it filled my ears. My cocoon of water had been interrupted by the rhythmic sound of a single paddle. I looked over my shoulder to see a red wooden canoe gliding through the water beside me. It was beautiful, meticulously maintained though it was obviously fifty-plus years old. The gloss of its many layers of paint made it look regal, not like the dull fiberglass canoes Pat and I had seen on Lake Louise. Those were canoes for tourists who wanted to float around and snap pictures. This was a genuine wooden canoe, made by craftsmen who had lovingly given it artful curves and lines. It had a new coat of varnish on all its wood, which gleamed as it slid over the water with a smooth *swoop, swoosh* of the paddle. It was as though every coat of paint had added to its depth and luster.

I watched it a long time until the red, sleek shape had been snapped into my memory—like a ballet dancer gracefully floating over an old stage floor or a Warhol painting popping off a beige gallery wall.

The red canoe reminded me of what God was doing with my life. It seemed the wood held a lifetime of stories, and with its layers of paint and care it looked ready to glide into the next fifty years.

The canoe made me think about the many gracious gifts God had given me in the last year. He had taught me how to navigate. I thought back to my first navigation lesson when I was fourteen. My dad demonstrated how to use a compass to lightly pencil a line showing our journey from place to place. He showed me how to consult tide charts, predict currents, and plan for channel depths. It was a lesson that taught me more than how to sail from one point to the next. It taught me that we are always at some point in our course. Some of us are staring blindly from the shoreline, others have just gotten on board, and still others are out in rough water. I have also come to believe that whether or not we know it, and whether or not we are willing participants, we are all on an adventure—headed toward a destination.

As I floated in Seely Lake, I couldn't help but think that without the stretching of our hearts, the drawn, ragged edge of ourselves, and our personal revelations of courage, we would not be able to tell where we were on our journey or to savor the destination with the same verve.

"It's the bitter that makes the sweet even sweeter," a friend used to say.

I confess to you now that I used to roll my eyes.

Today I see the truth in this idea that in life, any adventure must have certain elements. There must be the bitter—a crushing disappointment, a challenge, a time of personal conflict, an opportunity for courage—to appreciate the sweet destination.

Navigating begins first with the recognition that we are all somewhere on God's chart. This assures us that we are never really lost. I used to panic when I got lost while driving. Being lost would totally fry my entire composure to a frazzle. I would arrive in a sweaty froth, feeling stupid.

One day I was with a friend who was equally directionally challenged, but when he missed a turn, instead of getting flustered, he remarked, "Well, I guess we are on an adventure."

We were. Eventually we got where we were going, but the condition we arrived in was quite different. We were laughing and eager to tell everyone about our wrong turn in the road and where it had taken us.

Our perspective changes when we identify the wrong turns, the roadblocks, our fears, and even the enemy as part of a grand adventure. They are part of the plot in our story. This concept of an adventure allows me to relax. I can expect those wrong turns to fit in with the story line instead of ruining the ending.

This, I realized, is the perspective of buoyancy—and its benefit is not letting go to aimlessly float but letting go and learning to let God navigate our lives.

Some of us may feel like we are traveling in uncharted territory. We may feel like no one has been here before. I remember thinking, *No one could possibly know what this is like.*

I was wrong.

God saw me and he sees you. He is in the business of convincing us that we are unsinkable, valuable, strong. He is in the process of repainting our canoes—first sanding off the edges until the wood is clean and smooth so the beauty of our lives will reflect him. He is teaching us to chart our course and to glide in confidence. I believe he wants us to see that P31 exists in you and in me and in all the other women who find their compass in the words of a living Christ.

What would it be like to sit with the diva of the Proverbs in a Starbucks today? Would she be dressed in jeans and a T-shirt that reads WORLD'S GREATEST GRANDMA? Would her right arm be covered in silver bracelets that ring musically with the turn of her wrist? Would her dark hair be interrupted dramatically with a stripe of pure white—the kiss of a long life—and her dark skin and eyes only accentuate the effect?

This is how I see her.

"My name is Sophie," she would say and nod to the one empty chair in the place, welcoming me to join her for this little luxury in the day—a cuppa something with frothed milk before more craziness.

She would no doubt ask me if I'm just another *meshugine*, another crazy person who thinks I understand her life.

I'd tell her that I'm beginning to suspect that her life is not so different from my own—that she's not the superwoman myth I've bought into, championing her family, a clothing line, and the needs of a community all at the same time.

Putting her hand to her forehead, she'd laugh, take a sip of her own cup of Starbucks, and say, "Who does all these things in one day? These *shikses*, these non-Jewish women maybe?" She'd sigh, "They don't listen. They give me nothing but *tsures*."

My look of confusion would stop her.

"They give me nothing but trouble," she'd explain. She'd be quiet a second, taking another sip. "They don't get it."

"So what do you want women to get?" I'd ask her.

"I too have been a woman who sometimes doubted God," she'd say. "I had days I wanted to end. I had days I didn't want to begin. Laundry got in my way too. I never aspired to greatness or perfection. I just tried my best."

We'd be quiet a minute, and then she'd add, "That's what I wish women would get—that trying every morning, every moment counts. Not striving, but hoping and just living that hope."

This would make me smile, and she would know how much I'd want to share this.

"Yes," she'd smile and laugh. "Yes, do tell—tell your friends to get on with their own journeys instead of worrying about trying to follow mine."

As I lay in the lake floating near shore, I stretched my arms out and lay my hands palm up like a lily floating in the water. Somewhere between the place of imagining and just sheer happiness, I heard a woman's voice whisper in my head, "Kathy, what would *you* like them to get?"

I heard myself call back to her, "That I was a woman who found buoyancy, even in hard times, even when the water was over my head."

And then the picture rises slowly and makes its way to my brain: A red canoe held in stillness on a clear blue Montana Lake.

ACKNOWLEDGMENTS

I am thankful for my husband, Pat Vick, who not only makes my writing possible but is my biggest fan.

I am indebted to my family for allowing me to tell our story and face the hair-pulling event of a book deadline by putting up with frozen entrées and my occasional poor humor.

I am fortunate to have great friends who offered invaluable input into this book, and I am grateful for and humbled by their generosity: Karen Sjoblom, who has given me countless hours of friendship, encouragement, and inspiration; Kristin Jones, who faithfully read chapters in the middle of finals and cups at Starbucks; Cathy Eckard, who thinks I'm smarter than I really am; and Lindsey Smith, who read the first chapters of this book at 3:00 A.M. on a plane ride while six months pregnant. You are all my heroes.

Thank you, God, for graciously giving me Vivianna, my other mother, a siren, and a friend.

I am deeply grateful to Jeanette Thomason, Twila Bennett, and Wendy Wetzel for believing in this book.

God has brought many cherished mentors into my life. Among them are Bill and Nancie Carmichael, Dave and Claudia Arp, and Dr. Mary Mann Simon.

Finally, I am forever grateful to my sister, Cindee Sparks, who always told the other kids I was just big-boned and protected me with her life. You are a great woman and a wonderful sister. I love you.

Kathy Vick is an artist, writer, and designer who lives in Beaverton, Oregon, with her husband, Pat, and their son and daughter, Patrick and Andrea.

Kathy has worked in Christian publishing since 1981 on multiple projects including Christian magazines, radio, websites, women's and family ministries, and organizations featuring family seminars.

She's held titles from artist, designer, and art director to marketing director, editorial board member, book contributor, and author for Cook Communications Ministries, *Aspire, Virtue, Christian Parenting Today, Guideposts,* Effective Families Ministries, and Sunset, a megachurch along the Willow Creek model in Portland, Oregon. She currently works as a freelance designer and writer for multiple companies, including Left Coast Design.

Her passion is writing for and about women, which she began with magazine articles and book contributions in 1993. She writes from her life experience and on the premise—her life's philosophy—that God speaks to us in the details of the ordinary and that every woman is a secret weapon in his hands.

She and her husband enjoy road trips, fly fishing, motorcycling, and good barbeque; they delight in the uniqueness of their children.